How the Rich and Smart Break Free

Skills to Overcome Fear, Small Thinking and Dark Resistance—and Create Wealth

from GetTheBigYES.com

Tom Marcoux

Spoken Word Strategist
Executive Coach – Pitch Coach
Speaker-Author of 47 books
CEO

A QuickBreakthrough Publishing Edition

Other Books by Tom Marcoux:
• What the Rich Don't Say about Getting Rich
• Soar with Confidence: Pitch – Lead – Succeed
• Time Management Secrets the Rich Won't Tell You
• Relax, You Don't Need to Sell (Make Sales without Being Pushy) … with Authentic Marketing
• Dark Arts Defense Against Toxic People
• Darkest Secrets of Charisma
• Secrets of Awesome Dinner Guests: Walt Disney, Steve Jobs …
• Amazing You … featuring Secrets of Extreme Confidence
• Darkest Secrets of Persuasion and Seduction Masters
• Darkest Secrets of Making a Pitch to the Film / TV Industry

Praise for *How the Rich and Smart Break Free*

• "Tom Marcoux masterfully brings to light the things that no one is talking about. He gives you so many face-palm moments so you get your life back, and you unlock your true potential. Get this book." – Sean Douglas, TEDx Speaker, Author, Founder of The Success Corps

• "This book helps you become strong and mindful about how negative people and their tactics affect us. And it offers ways to build an immunity toward negative people and 'well-intentioned saboteurs.' You'll learn to build and sustain a powerful motivation to keep focused and achieve your dreams." – David Barron, Author, Hypnotist, founder of New Hampshire Hypnosis, newhampshirehypnosis.com

Praise for Tom Marcoux's Other Work:

• "Concerned about networking situations? Get *Relax Your Way Networking*. Success is built on high trust relationships. Master Coach Tom Marcoux reveals secrets to increase your influence."
– Greg S. Reid, Author, *Think and Grow Rich Series*

• "In Tom Marcoux's *Now You See Me*, the powerful and easy-to-use ideas can make a big difference in your business and your personal relationships."
– Allen Klein, author of *You Can't Ruin My Day*

• "In *Darkest Secrets of Persuasion and Seduction Masters: How to Protect Yourself and Turn the Power to Good*, learn useful countermeasures to protect you from being darkly manipulated."
– David Barron, co-author, *Power Persuasion*

• "In *Connect*, Tom's advice on how to remain true to yourself and establish authentic rapport with clients is both insightful and reality based. He [shows how] to establish oneself as a credible expert."
– Arthur P. Ciaramicoli, Ed.D., Ph.D., author *The Stress Solution*

• "In *Reduce Clutter, Enlarge Your Life*, Marcoux will help you get rid of the physical and mental clutter occupying precious space in your life. You'll reclaim wasted energy, lower your stress, and find time for new opportunities." – Laura Stack, author of *Execution IS the Strategy*

Visit Tom's blogs: GetTheBigYES.com   PitchPowerFest.com YourBodySoulandProsperity.com

CONTENTS*

* These are highlights. Much more is in this book.

DEDICATION AND ACKNOWLEDGMENTS

This work is dedicated to YOU. Here are Special Offers:

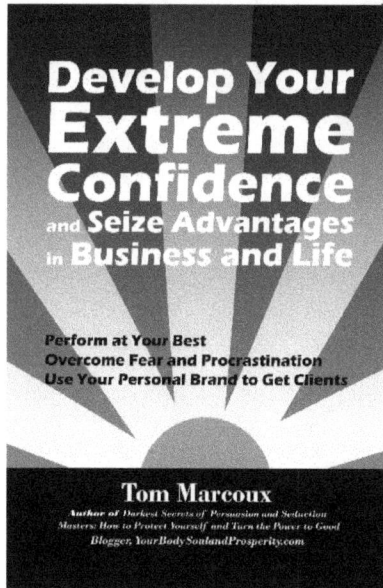

- Get your free eBook *Develop Your Extreme Confidence and Seize Advantages in Business and Life* at http://bit.ly/29bVpox
- Apply for a **Free Breakthrough Strategy Session** with Tom Marcoux https://tomsupercoach.com/breakthrough/

This book also dedicated to the terrific Video/Audio Strategist and author Johanna E. Mac Leod. Thanks to Kalen Vavla for editing a section. Thanks to Johanna E. Mac Leod for this book's cover. Thanks to my father, Al Marcoux, for his concern and efforts for me … and to my mother, Sumiyo Marcoux, a kind, generous soul. Thank you to Higher Power … and to our readers, audiences, clients, my graduate students and my team members of Tom Marcoux Media, LLC and GetTheBigYES.com. The best to you.

How the Rich and Smart Defeat Dark Tactics and Create Wealth

What do you really want? Have you found your way to create riches and happiness in your life?

If you have put in significant effort to increase your financial abundance, *you have probably run into blocks and sabotage*—like my client, Trudy, who said, "I just can't believe this. My own friends and family are sabotaging my efforts to make my business work. Am I making too big a deal of this?"

"I've listened carefully to you in the recent sessions. You're *not* exaggerating. We need to make you strong and alert," I said.

This began a significant discussion that included alerting Trudy to **Dark Tactics**, and those people in her life who were causing damage.

If you want to be rich, you cannot be normal. – Noah St. John

I'll say it in few words:
To be rich, you must defeat Dark Tactics.

Who uses Dark Tactics against you?
- Manipulators
- Toxic People (subset: Crazy-makers)
- Well-Intentioned Saboteurs*

* A Well-Intentioned Saboteur is someone who thinks they're doing you a service, but they are killing your dreams. They try to protect you, but they stunt your growth.

We will empower you, so you avoid succumbing to **Dark Tactics:**

D – declare that accumulation of wealth and use of persuasion are wrong
A – abuse and brainwash you to *not* grow
R – require you to stay small or they withdraw approval
K – kill your ideas

In this book, we will cover *Countermeasures.* The Countermeasure to "Declare that accumulation of wealth and use of persuasion are wrong" is *Develop lots of evidence that you're making progress.*

Dark Tactics form a subset of what I call **Dark Resistance.**

Some highlights from this book:
- Use Leverage for Wealth
- The Power of Fearless vs. Self-Doubt
- Create Your Personal Brand—for Success
- Make Great Decisions When Facing Risk
- Network for Clients, Contacts and Friends
- Warm Up Relationships with Humor (How to Be Funny)
- How to Use Your Intuition Well

- Convince Investors to Fund You: Master the 3 Critical Factors of Pitch, Network and Follow-Up
- The Savvy CEO Wins

You can increase your income. You need to learn the strategies, and **you'll dig deeper than before and do what you've never done.**

If you have a lousy attitude, you'll see obstacles as threats and annoyances. If you have a positive attitude, you'll see obstacles as interesting or even fun. – Geoffrey James

Through this book, I am your Executive Coach.
Let's get started.

A Special Note: When I share details about Dark Resistance with a client or an audience, I point out: "When you want to do something extraordinary, you'll likely get surprised by the *resistance* you get from friends and family. It often takes the form of a comment or action that drains your personal power. To take away someone's personal power—and kill their dreams—is dark. Hence, I call it **Dark Resistance.**

Dark Tactic #1

Declare that Accumulation of Wealth and Use of Persuasion Are Wrong

Countermeasure: *Develop lots of evidence that you're making progress.*

What's keeping you from being rich? In most cases it's simply a lack of belief. In order to become rich, you must believe you can do it, and you must take the actions necessary to achieve your goal.
– Suze Orman

Many of us grew up in a household that included a parent or guardian who refused to talk about money, or they merely complained about money. Worse, they stated that one had to do something wrong or evil to gain money. This point of view is like pouring concrete on the head of a young person.

This makes the young person stuck instead of inspiring them to learn to be creative and solve problems. People with tough problems often will gladly pay for solutions.

One of the reasons I'm writing this book is that I feel deep concern and sometimes some anger toward the practice of shooting down people's ideas, hopes and real potential to take action and do extraordinary things.

Complaining about money is ordinary.

To get rich, you can't be normal. – Noah St. John

You're going to hear a lot of theories about how to become wealthy, mostly from people who have never done it. ... The fact is that most people don't have the ambition or the guts to go out and stake their claim, and when you do, they get jealous. Your success becomes a mirror and when they look, they don't like what they see. It's easier to demonize the rich than it is to become one of them. ... Study the most successful self-made millionaires, and you'll find a substantial trail of satisfied customers. – Steve Siebold

As an executive coach and the Spoken Word Strategist, I help people break down barriers and experience creative freedom.

Brad Carlson, one of my clients, said, "Tom Marcoux coached me to get more done in 10 days than other coaches in 2 years." I share this here because it's an expression of evidence.

On the other hand, several authors put an extreme emphasis on "rah-rah positive self-talk." Some would say that you could get yourself into action by telling yourself "I feel terrific."

I've encountered a significant number of people who say "Positive affirmations don't work. I just feel like I'm lying to myself."

Working with clients, I help people with what I call *Behavior Change through Incremental Evidence.* I have observed that focusing on your *Words – Strategy – Rehearsal* gives one evidence that you're becoming more skillful.

I emphasize that the Countermeasure to Dark Tactic #1 "Declare that the accumulation of wealth and use of persuasion are wrong" is to *develop lots of evidence that you're making progress.*

By this I mean, you demonstrate to yourself that you are doing positive things, helping people accomplish their goals, and naturally your income increases.

Beware of the Toxic Ideas from Toxic People

To go against the prejudices of parents or guardians or to make more money than them may take *a lot of inner strength.* I have heard clients tell me that their parents said that it does not matter about fulfilling commitments to clients. What?!

This is important. We're talking about being trustworthy and fulfilling your promises.

Then some of these parents or guardians say it does not matter whether you take care of yourself and make sure you get enough rest and recovery. It is strange to hear that a loved one does not care if you protect your job or your own business.

What is going on here?

These individuals are toxic people. Toxic people are truly self-centered.

The answer is: *Reduce your exposure to them.*

One of my editors said, "This makes no sense. How can somebody who supposedly loves you be so against your health and happiness?"

"Great question," I replied. "This is just another example of what some researchers call 'crazy-making.' What's even worse is that a good person will feel guilty for not visiting their parents who are so mean."

The truth is that humans often act in illogical ways. A major problem about interacting with crazy-makers is that **they have no empathy.** If you pay close attention, you realize that there is no "solution." You can be nice. You can take the abuse. You can stand your ground and say, "You're insulting me" or "Stop being so mean."

And what outcome do you get? Does the crazy-maker care? No.

I once said to one of my older relatives, "You're not listening to me. Do you want to listen to me?"

"No," was the crazy-maker's reply.

So, what do you do?

You acknowledge reality.

One tough truth to notice is that *if you make efforts to be rich, some people in your circle will actively (or even subtly) take action to tear you down.*

Acknowledge the reality and quietly (in your own mind and with your own actions) defend yourself. Defend your well-being and your wealth-accumulating process.

Develop Your Own Healthy Approach to Persuasion

Perhaps, you heard a family member say things like:
- We can't afford that.
- Every fortune is built on a crime.
- Rich people are evil. Rich people are heartless.
- I hate salespeople!

Now is the time for you to free yourself from shackles—in your thinking and in your actions.

To overcome "Declare that the accumulation of wealth and the use of persuasion are wrong," we need something strong. We need to develop lots of evidence that you're making progress. **Evidence can be stronger than the lies or limiting beliefs that swim in our subconscious mind.**

Billions of people ... have subconscious negative programming that is causing them to short-circuit and self-sabotage their own success. ... In any conflict between the conscious and subconscious mind, the subconscious always wins. ... Most of the memes floating around the globe ... create and/or reinforce negative, limiting beliefs that are not in your highest good. And a huge proportion of the most powerful and prevalent mind viruses in the world today revolve around money and success—including Money is evil, Rich people are bad. – Randy Gage

Now is the time to make your own choice. Develop your own healthy approach to persuasion.

I wrote a whole book on sales and something even better "enrollment" titled, *Relax You Don't Have to Sell: How to Make Sales without Being Pushy.* This book was the required textbook when I taught MBA students in my class Authentic Marketing.

Here I'll share a few insights about getting rich and being adept with sales and persuasion.

1) Many people destroy their opportunities for great wealth because they confuse persuasion with manipulation. Numerous times, I have explained to various audiences (and classes of MBA students) that we can have useful, operational definitions of persuasion and manipulation.

Persuasion – you begin with the well-being of the person in mind and you help them get what will enhance their life.

Manipulation – someone has *no regard* for the person's well-being, and they merely pull strings on that person to get something (money, influence, etc.) from that person.

Holding a positive intention to support the person's well-being makes it possible to ethically and effectively persuade with skill and ease. Your intention is a vital component of this whole process.

2) Training in sales and enrollment are vital elements so you can increase your value to the marketplace.

Everything about my journey to get Spanx off the ground entailed me having to be a salesperson—from going to the hosiery mills to get a prototype made to calling Saks Fifth Avenue and Neiman Marcus. I had to position myself to get five minutes in the door with buyers. – Sara Blakely

3) You can learn to do a powerful and ethical process of selling.

Just because most don't make it doesn't mean you can't.
– Grant Cardone

4) If someone accuses you of selling, you can reply in a positive manner. You could say, "Oh, was there something valuable that's come up in our conversation? I'm all about making sure people get what they want."

The ambitious are criticized by those that have given up.
– Grant Cardone

5) You can learn to be skillful when talking about fees and the value you provide.*

When training my clients in how to talk about their fees, I help them realize that when the other person questions the fee, that person is (in a way) asking: "Would you show vividly where the value for me is in this thing?"

6) Any hesitation in learning how to ethically and effective sell and use appropriate persuasion often connects with a general discomfort about money.

To gain clarity and move forward, I developed my own intention around money: *Money is a tool I use well for the benefit of all involved.*

* For an empowering discussion about effective selling and "enrolling" see my book, *Relax You Don't Have to Sell.*

Power Principle:
Develop lots of evidence that you're making progress.

Power Questions:
How are you devoting effort to release yourself from limiting beliefs as you make incremental progress? What kinds of beliefs are people with no relevant experience foisting upon you? How are you pressing forward regardless of such limiting beliefs? How are you getting the coaching and training to be effective with sales and persuasion?

Tom Marcoux

Dark Tactic #2

Abuse and Brainwash You to *Not* Grow

Countermeasure: *Make the choice and take action to place positive inputs into your mind.*

The common mindset of the masses is fear and scarcity.... The main reason that so few people transcend this fear-based mindset is due primarily to its pervasiveness. When everyone around you is operating from fear and scarcity, it's contagious. – Steve Siebold

A successful [person] is one who can lay a firm foundation with the bricks others have thrown at him. – David Brinkley

Do you feel that in some way you were brainwashed to think that you had to stay stuck where you are? A friend of mine said that parents and guardians have "echoes of diapers." By this he meant that parents and guardians have memories of us as children. The whole point is that **we are supposed to grow out of our childish ways.** We're supposed to grow into our own destiny.

Our destiny can be far different than the destiny of our parents or guardians. I chose the word *abuse* with care. I had been on the receiving end of a father who threw me into walls and spit in my face. That was only the physical abuse. The verbal abuse and the limiting beliefs that he worked to shove in my brain caused pain and trouble for me.

At 15, I made a significant decision upon realizing that my father's love for me was conditional. At that moment I had a choice: turn bitter or I could decide to listen to my own inner voice about my own destiny. Some years later, I would write in a book: *Measure by your heart, not their approval.*

As I wrote the book, I realized that my father had given me a backhanded gift: By not giving me approval, the door was open for me to seek to listen to my inner true self.

If plan A fails, remember there are 25 more letters.
– Chris Guillebeau

If you don't value your time, neither will others. Stop giving away your time and talents. Value what you know and start charging for it. – Kim Garst

Beware of a Certain Form of Toxic People —The Crazy-makers

Crazy-makers come in all shapes and sizes—and can have good and bad intentions. Some know they are being manipulative and oppressive. Others haven't got a clue. Some engage in their tactics consistently. Others provide intermittent surprise attacks. The challenge is to recognize the behavior, assess if it's from a healthy or unhealthy place, and then employ the proper strategies to stay sane and empower yourself. ... The Top 3 Crazy-maker Types are narcissists, drama-cultivators and stealth-bombers. ... Crazy-

makers cannot empathize. – Kimberly Key

While I was writing this book, two people did some crazy-maker-actions that hurt two people close to me. I took this as a sign that the universe was inviting me to include the Crazy-maker (a form of toxic person) in this book.

In few words, Crazy-makers use Dark Tactics, and you cannot change their behavior by using gentle responses.

We note that you cannot change a Crazy-maker, but in certain circumstances you can change what you do and create consequences the Crazy-maker does not like.

Will that get you cooperation? No guarantees.

What works is to *Reduce Your Exposure* to crazy-makers. Put a container around the damage their trying to cause.

This section notes: "Abuse and brainwash you to *not* grow."

Resolve to empower yourself to grow. When you know a crazy-maker will verbally shoot down your efforts and dreams, inoculate yourself. Empower yourself. Be sure to put positive inputs in your mind. Here are helpful quotes:

Everything is theoretically impossible, until it is done.
– Robert A. Heinlein

If you think you're too small to have an impact, try going to bed with a mosquito. – Anita Roddick

Beware that People Who Love You Can Bury You in Sabotaging Thoughts

Most of us want to tell our coworkers or friends, or husbands or wives, our ideas. For what reason? We want validation. But I feel ideas are most vulnerable in their infancy. Out of love and concern, friends and family give all the reasons or objections on why you shouldn't do it. I didn't want to risk that. – Sara Blakely

When you have an idea with a good potential, you need to be your own best advocate. Your friends and family, who care about you, still are **not** able experience the comfort of your vision. It is *not* their destiny. They cannot feel real enthusiasm that resides in your heart.

Power Principle:
Make the choice and take action to place positive inputs into your mind.

Power Questions:
What abusive thoughts are some people foisting upon you? How are you reducing your exposure to the energy-draining people you encounter? How are you taking consistent action for have positive inputs into your mind?

Dark Tactic #3

Require You to Stay Small or
They Withdraw Approval

Countermeasure: *Identify who lifts you and reduce exposure to anyone who treads on you. Empower yourself.*

No person is your friend who demands your silence or denies your right to grow. – Alice Walker

Have you noticed that some people, even friends, *act like snipers* against your hopeful ideas and intent to provide great service and earn financial abundance?

Years ago, I said to a friend: "I'm concerned. I've seen you drop friends. I have a feeling that when I hit a home run financially, you'll make up some reason to be angry at me — and you'll leave."

This friend did *not* say anything. He did *not* reassure me at all.

This person is *not* in my life, anymore. What a relief! I recovered so much time. As a good friend, I would check in with this person and do so much listening.

The person did me a favor by drifting away.

Now it's your turn. **Who would do you a favor if they drifted out of your life? Who requires you to stay small?**

Pay close attention. Identify who in your life says that they're not interested in your working with ideas. Do they also subtly tear apart your plans to solve people's problems and earn financial abundance? Reduce your exposure to such people.

I surround myself with good people who make me feel great and give me positive energy. – Ali Krieger

Picture a bucket filed with crabs. One individual crab wants to leave and to rise above. As the one crab (our hero) strives to leave, the other crabs reach up and drag that crab down. This is an example of what's called "The Crab Mentality."

It's important for you to identify those crabs in your life who are *not* for you. The sad thing is some of these people might be close friends or even family members.

These people often use the Dark Tactic of *requiring you to stay small or they withdraw approval.* Don't let someone else with their own small ideas and small life control you through their use of withdrawing approval. I've written in my books: **Measure by your heart, and not their approval.**

To succeed you have to believe in something with such a passion that it becomes a reality. – Anita Roddick

You can help a thousand. But you cannot carry three on your back. – Jim Rohn

Often, a person who dedicates themselves to making a positive impact and creating personal financial abundance, will receive *significant resistance.*

You will need to listen to your heart. You must move beyond an understandable desire for approval.

Your thinking will need to be strong and independent. I have often noted that Walt Disney had to stay strong when everyone (his wife, business partner and brother Roy O. Disney, the board of directors) were all against Disneyland.

To get rich, you need to empower yourself to think of the extraordinary—the nonlinear solutions.

Creating linear solutions will make you a living. Creating nonlinear solutions will make you rich. – Steve Siebold

It was never about attaining wealth or celebrity. It was about the process of continually seeking to be better, to challenge myself to pursue excellence on every level. – Oprah Winfrey

Power Principle:
Identify who lifts you and *reduce exposure to anyone who treads on you.* Empower yourself.

Power Questions:
Who is acting like a sniper who shoots down your ideas before you have the chance to develop them and test them? How can you reduce exposure to such people? What will you do to keep stretching and testing ideas with potential?

Tom Marcoux

Dark Tactic #4

Kill Your Ideas

Countermeasure: *Protect the Talent and guard your momentum.*

When someone shows you who they are, believe them the first time. – Maya Angelou

"What just happened?" a friend asked me.

"That's just what he does," I explained about one of my family members. "Around him, it's where good ideas go to die."

I learned to keep my fledgling ideas to myself and away from this family member.

One year, I asked this family member: "You're not listening to me. Do you want to listen to me?"

He said, "No."

That gave me the opportunity to implement the wisdom behind Maya Angelou's comment: *"When someone shows you who they are, believe them the first time."*

On the other hand, I learned to develop a whole circle of

people who provide helpful feedback. As I was developing an idea for a TED Talk, I gained feedback from 12 people in succession.

Let's think about this for a moment. If somebody kills your ideas, they can be actually killing a part of you. It's been said that you can always replace money, but you can't replace time. If somebody wastes your time or somebody kills one of your good ideas that has potential, that person is destroying something precious.

Don't let that happen.

All achievements, all earned riches, have their beginning in an idea. –Napoleon Hill

Thought is the original source of all wealth, all success, all material gain, all great discoveries and inventions, and of all achievement. – Claude M. Bristol

When a person has an idea, at that conception moment it is the most vulnerable—one negative comment could knock you off course. – Sara Blakely

"What did you learn as a feature film director, Tom?" I was asked in a recent interview.

"Protect the Talent and guard momentum," I replied. I explained that in the film industry "the talent" refers to male and female actors. When I'm directing a feature film, I make sure that the actors have some place where they can rest. Meanwhile, the stand-ins help the cinematographer and crew by holding their positions. People lose energy by just standing in place. So, the stand-ins have a vital role to perform. All the lights, writing and camerawork mean nothing if the Talent are not fully alive and able to give a great performance.

When you treat yourself like The Talent, you make sure that you rest, recover and reserve your energy for the most important tasks and moments.

Additionally, you protect yourself and your ideas, which have the potential to create great service that earns great wealth.

All of the great ideas, without action, become stale and useless. The key to turning dreams into reality is action. People who have great ideas are a dime a dozen. People who act on their dreams and ideas are the select few, but they are the ones who gain the health, wealth and wisdom that is available. Someone will act today. Let it be you. – Jim Rohn

Profits are better than wages. Wages make you a living; profits make you a fortune. – Jim Rohn.

A wage is earned hour by hour. There is a ceiling to this.

Massive wealth is often earned through implementing a good idea.

Be alert to identifying who gives you constructive feedback that helps you improve your performance. Be sure to know who is giving you "garbage."

When I say garbage, I mean offering an opinion that is *not* backed up relevant experience and is merely a reflex version of negativity and naysaying.

Running a company on market research is like driving while looking in the rear-view mirror. – Anita Roddick

Speed, agility and responsiveness are the keys to future success. – Anita Roddick

Stay Alert for When to Go with a "Bold" Idea

The word 'Spanx' was funny. It made people laugh. No one ever forgot it. – Sara Blakely

Beware of experts who say, "You can't do that." They may be only looking in the rearview mirror.

When I work with clients, I'm in this present moment. For example, I wrote a phrase for one client: "You're stressed out because your systems suck." I confirmed with him that I had captured his style and his voice.

When I started to describe my work as "the Spoken Word Strategist and Executive Coach," certain individuals said, "Pick one. You must choose one."

"No, I don't. These two facets fit me," I replied.

Now it's your turn. Do you have a "bold idea"? No one knows how the marketplace will respond.

Set something up so people can *vote with their wallets.*

Can you release a version of your product? In some cases, people can use something like Kickstarter.com to see if people will put down money to contribute to a product being made. For example, my sweetheart put down money for a small aquarium that that used gases from the excretions of the fish to fertilize a plant (set at the surface of the water). The fish, water and plant formed an interesting eco-system. My sweetheart put money down and received the aquarium a few months later. A successful Kickstarter.com campaign.

This was a true demonstration of how to be sure that your idea is viable in the marketplace.

Make Your Ideas Thrive Without Others' Approval

We do not need to despair if we experience fear, anger, or sadness. In fact, they are crucial. They become problematic only when they become imbalanced—when our fear tips into paralysis, when our anger tips into rage, when our sadness tips into despair. The key is to DEFEND ourselves against the forces that conspire to push us over that edge. – Shawn Achor

Sometimes, you must *press on and defend* your heart and your ideas.

I'd really like it if my sweetheart would find my entrepreneurial ideas to be spot on and to her liking.

Sometimes, she does *not* like my creative ideas. Okay.

Walt Disney found that his wife, brother Roy O. Disney (his business partner) and the board of directors were all *against* Disneyland. Walt did *not* let that stop him.

As I was writing a version of my first book in my *Jenalee Storm* series, my sweetheart didn't like how the book idea was changing. I'd prefer that she like my work. That's the vital word, *prefer*.

I kept writing, and, as a bonus, she now likes my series of novels titled *Jenalee Storm* (that I write with a pen name). It's a bonus.

I've learned along the way that you must listen to your own heart. My phrase is: **Measure by your heart, not their approval.**

Solve a big problem, and the world will gladly turn their money over to you. … The larger problem you solve, the richer you get.
– Steve Siebold

All riches have their origin in mind. Wealth is in ideas—not money. – Robert Collier

To be wealthy you must develop a burning desire for wealth and financial independence. – Brian Tracy

It's how you deal with failure that determines how you achieve success. – David Feherty

Power Principle:
Protect the Talent and guard your momentum.

Power Questions:
How are you protecting your personal energy? Have you identified other people or your own personal habits that sabotage your momentum? What are you doing to guard your momentum?

Next Sections of this Book:

- The Power of Fearless vs. Self-Doubt
- Create Your Personal Brand—for Success
- Make Great Decisions When Facing Risk
- Network for Clients, Contacts and Friends
- Warm Up Relationships with Humor (How to Be Funny)
- How to Use Your Intuition Well
- Use Leverage for Wealth
- Convince Investors to Fund You: Master the 3 Critical Factors of Pitch, Network and Follow-Up
- The Savvy CEO Wins

The Power of Fearless vs. Self-Doubt

The biggest obstacle to wealth is fear. People are afraid to think big, but if you think small, you'll only achieve small things.
– T. Harv Eker

My first account was Neiman Marcus. I cold-called them just like I had cold-called businesses when I was selling fax machines for seven years. – Sara Blakely

What is "fearless"?

There's a lot that bothers us—a lot of pain and imposition of forces on people, economic and otherwise.

It's understandable that so many of us feel boxed in by fear.

I gave this a lot of thought. Can you ever really be fearless?

Unless you're a monk who meditates for six hours a day, it's likely that you have fearful thoughts several times per week.

 The idea is that a monk, eventually through tens of hours of meditation, faces all the fear and becomes able to move into a place of calm contemplation.

I do some meditation, but I do not do it for six hours. So, you're probably like me, and you face fear on many occasions.

How can we get to the level of fearless?

Look at the word *fearless.* The idea is for you to have some experiences of *less* fear. Imagine having a moment in which fear is a quieter voice. Fear may be on the committee, but it's not running the show. The CEO of your show is your true self, not the fear part.

How *fearless* is attractive

I've been through some really rough times. As a child I had a father who threw me into walls and spit on me. In my early years, I had been around or been pulled into violent situations. So, I'm talking about real times where I've felt full of fear. Of course, that makes it attractive for me to get to a place of *fear less.*

I learned that getting free of fear is not about "rah-rah positive self-talk." You could say, "I feel terrific," but there's a part of you that says, "No, you don't." So, that feels like a lie.

What's the solution? It's having a pragmatic system.

It became my personal mission to come up with systems, so I can be massively productive. One of my mentors said, "Make sure to put out *massive high-quality output.*"

I learned that I wanted to be strong and to be able to take appropriate risks—*and* in my true self feel some safety. I developed a system built around the word S.A.F.E.

We use the S.A.F.E. process:

S – set a system
A – ask a question
F – focus
E – empower your second thought

1. Set a system

A system is much better than trying to rely on willpower. I know this for a fact. In the morning I can eat well and eat spinach. But At 2 AM, I'm not in the mood to eat spinach. I'm more in the mood to eat cookies. *I use a system. I declare that I'm going to eat one lemon Oreo cookie.*

When I mention this, some people reply, "I have to limit myself to one *row* of Oreo cookies."

The problem is: as the day goes on, our willpower wears out—like a muscle succumbing to fatigue.

As I mentioned, my system is to *declare* I get one lemon Oreo cookie. Now, I'm going to live up to my declaration.

An Answer for "How do you keep the system from derailing?"

You prepare that there will be some stumbles or backsliding. Set up backup systems. If one is an engineer, you have failsafe mechanisms. You know certain things are going to happen.

For example, for anyone who is wanting to eat in a truly healthy way, you need to have a plan or system for the times you might falter. If you have more than one cookie, do *not* give up on the whole day. That is, do not tell yourself, "Okay. The door is open. I'll eat anything now."

Be aware that people tend to fall back. They tend to have setbacks. So, instead of just throwing up your hands and saying, "well there goes the whole day," you have a plan that includes adding a second walk into that day—for example.

The way to avoid being derailed from your goal is to set up supporting details. Have a backup system.

Systems are a crucial foundation for acting in a fearless way—with fear as a quiet voice in the background.

For example, I recently wrote my 46th book, *The Writer's*

Solution—Crush Your Self-Doubt. While writing the book, I got stuck. I felt some fear.

Then, I relied on my system of *3 Vital Questions:*

a) Am I telling the truth? – Yes.

b) Can this book help someone? – Yes.

c) Can I express this in a brief and clear way? – Yes.

So, I did not let fear stop me. I worked efficiently. I went from idea to finished book on a major retailer's website in 61 days.

2. Ask a question

Some people get stuck in writing a book because they're afraid that their first book may fail to sell a lot of copies. Then their fear intensifies with this idea: "No publisher will want to publish a book by an author who only sold 500 copies."

Now it's time to ask a question to challenge one's assumptions.

Is it possible that a publisher could assess that your next book is fresh and that it will make money? Is that possible? Because there have been publishers who have published books by unproven authors based on specific factors like: "It's fresh, controversial—it will make money."

My point here is that it's important to question one's first assumptions.

Consider asking:

- Is that true?
- How do I know that's true?
- Has anyone ever succeeded at this?
- What could I do to make myself stretch and try something different and bring something fresh to the marketplace?

Questions can get you out of a loop of ruminating over bad outcomes.

3. Focus

Consider this:

When you're in action, you're focused, and fear is a quiet voice in the background.

My point is "fearless" means "less fear—and fear does *not* run your life."

Still, fear is *not* always a bad thing.

Fear helps you stay on the mountain. For example, if somebody has no fear and they take no precautions, it's Ahhhh! Thud! An observer says, "They had no fear."

I reply: "But they felt that landing."

It's important to properly utilize fear as a member of your committee.

When fear transforms into "get ready energy" and rehearsal, there is less fear. This forms part of the essence of my work with my clients. We focus on *Words – Strategy – Rehearsal.*

I help the client *unleash from within* his or her words.

Some clients ask, "What do I do when I feel nervous?"

"If you're concerned about something, grab five minutes of rehearsal," I reply. "Call up a friend. Talk to them and say 'Hey do you have a minute? I just want to practice the beginning—the first two minutes of my speech.'"

Or call your own answering system and practice expressing your speech while your answering system records your message. This will help you transform fear into "get ready energy." And you'll develop some evidence that you've practiced. You're getting better. This is a part of a process that I help my clients experience. I call it: *Behavior Change through Incremental Evidence.*

I'm *not* interested in getting people to do "rah-rah, positive self-talk." I want them to see their progress. To feel in their body and mind, that they're getting prepared.

A powerful thing that I do with my clients is to help them *overprepare* for a speech. As I mentioned, we focus on Words – Strategy – Rehearsal.

Some of my new clients say, "I don't like to record my voice. I don't like the sound of my voice."

"I agree. I don't like the recorded sound of my voice, too," I reply.

This is also the same thing about people with their noses. I've only met two people in my whole life who like their noses. So, the reality of you not liking your own voice is just something that you must be prepared for. You'll likely be surprised by the sound of your recorded voice. Why? You're used to hearing your voice resonate from within your body. That's how it seems to have *more* resonance. Like many things, you can get used to it, if you record and listen to your voice enough times.

4. Empower your second thought

Here's an important point, in particular, for introverts. If you're an introvert, you probably have had a similar experience to what I've encountered.

My first thought at several times was "I have a disadvantage compared to extroverts." It looks like that they're having a great time. They *like* attending parties and networking events. What I've learned is that I need to move past that initial thought. I need to ask myself a question: "Can I pick a better thought to focus on?"

Then I decide to let go of the disempowering thought of "I'm an introvert and I'm at a disadvantage." I let that thought flow past—like it is a leaf on a stream of water.

Only by letting that first thought go, then I can get to my *Empowering Second Thought.*

Let a Disempowering Thought "Float By"

Unfortunately, a lot of us have almost a "reflex." We think a disempowering thought, but we have not practiced letting it pass by, like a leaf flowing on a stream.

Instead, we might take that leaf (that thought) and shove it right next to our eyes. And then we can't see anything else.

Aim to let that thought flow by.

You could simply ask, "What's another thought? Is there a better thought? What am I good at?

Let's say you're an introvert. Many introverts are good at thinking things through. So, before a networking event, preplan your questions. You could ask:

- How is this conference going for you?
- Are you looking forward to a particular speaker?
- Who is your ideal client? (You would ask this later in a conversation.)

At one conference of coaches and others who help people, my phrase was: "So, how do you help people?"

Here's how an introvert, Anita, uses the comfort she feels when talking with people one-to-one. Before she gives a speech, she makes sure to meet some audience members. In this way, she will have some friendly faces in the audience.

Pick three people to focus on—one to your right, another to your left and someone in the center. This helps your audience feel that you're including the whole room of attendees.

For an introvert, it works to think of a networking event

as the opportunity to do a lot of listening. If you think that all you must do is listen well, then you don't feel that you need to have as much energy. Introverts cannot rely on being able to ad-lib like an extravert. So, the idea is for the introvert to think things through (using the Introvert's Advantage) and come up with appropriate questions.

When Networking You Can Fall Back on "What are you looking forward to?"

People often ask, "About what? Work? A vacation?"

"Whatever you prefer to talk about," I reply.

Having *gentle questions* is a workable system. I define gentle questions in this situation as "questions that are easy and, at times, fun to answer." Talking about a pending vacation can be fun. Then the person feels good in your presence. Let's call that a win.

Four Things to Remember

As I mentioned, I emphasize S.A.F.E.

S stands for Set a System

Set a System because without a system you might fall back into the fear that having a low mood prevents you from getting something done. For example, many people experience fear and a block when they want to write. As I write these words, it's 4:35 A.M. I'm *not* in the mood to write. Often, I'm not in the mood to write, but I have a system. First, I know that I'll make a Progress Log entry. That will build up my morale. If I'm tired, I'll speak into my dictating app. I just record 30 words while my target is 2,000 words for that day. With 30 words done, I only have 970 more words to go. That's better than having done nothing.

That's **better than zero.**

A stands for Ask a Question

When a disempowering thought arises in your mind, ask yourself: "Is there another thought for me? Could I think of something that helps me take a small step forward?

F stands for Focus.

Focus on a small action that you can take. When you're in action, you're focused, and fear is a quiet voice in the background.

E stands for Empower Your Second Thought

Researchers have noticed that the negative experience goes straight into long-term memory. Why? You can blame it on our ancestors. Because the ones who lived were the ones who had negative thinking. "Oh, look that's a saber-tooth tiger. I'm getting out of here."

On the other hand, other individuals looked at a saber-tooth tiger and said, "Hello kitty." Those were the ones who did not live. They did not pass their genes down.

So, people living now are genetically predisposed to pay more attention to the negative.

Researchers note that we need to focus on a positive experience for 10 to 20 seconds, to place it into one's long-term memory. This detail caught my attention so much and I wrote a book titled, *10 Seconds to Wealth.*

Here's an example. If I cut myself shaving—boom, right into my long-term memory.

Here's what helps: *Choose to condition your mind to go to an Empowering Second Thought.* This process helps you move beyond negative thoughts.

I helped one client learn to shift out of her automatic negative thoughts. How? I invited her to immediately ask herself: "What is working in my life?" and "What small thing can I do to improve this situation?"

Power Principle:

When fear transforms into *get ready energy* and rehearsal, there is less fear.

Power Questions:

Are you looking at setting a system, so you can get the coaching and rehearsal to help you excel? Are you guarding yourself against distraction, so you can focus on what is most important? Have you begun to search for versions of a *second thought* that can help you move beyond a reflex-like negative first thought?

Make Great Decisions When Facing Risk

(A version of this material originally appeared at my blog GetTheBigYES.com)

"It's hard for me to make the big decisions," my client Cara said.

"I hear you," I replied. "That's understandable. I've been listening carefully to your current situation and you have a lot at stake."

Working with clients, and as CEO, leading my international team members for my own company, I work with people taking appropriate risks.

I recall this quote:

Failure or the risk of failure could often be a crucial step on the road to success. – Dominic Randolph

Being skillful about "risk of failure" is valuable.

The heart and soul of the company is creativity and innovation. ... People don't like to follow pessimists. – Bob Iger, CEO of The Walt Disney Company

I usually write about having courage and using strategy to take appropriate risks.

There is another side to this equation.

It's valuable to learn when taking a particular risk is ill-advised.

I use *3 Considerations Related to Saying "No" to a Particular Risk*

- "If It's not hell yes, then it's hell no."
- I don't feel a burning energy to do this.
- If in doubt, leave it out.
- Bonus Consideration: Really wanting it to be true does *not* make it true.

1. "If it's not hell yes, then it's hell no."

Years ago, I saw a comment by Cheryl Richardson in one of her books: "If it's not hell yes, then it's hell no."

This is useful. Why? Because whatever you decide, you're going to pay for it. For example, years ago, I directed a feature film in which I played a leading character and I did my own stunts.

I held onto the hood of a speeding, classic, cherry-red Chevy truck going 60 miles an hour.

Would I do that today? No. I'm not interested. Been there, done that. I'm older, and I'm not interested in risking great injury. I'd rather devote my time to writing several urban fantasy novels in my *Jenalee Storm* series (which is designed to blossom as episodes in some media—perhaps, Netflix). I lead my team of editors and book cover professionals), as I write *Jenalee Storm* under a pen name.

Now it's your turn. Do you really want something? Is it a total, enthusiastic "hell yes!"? If not, then maybe it's NOT worth it to you.

2. "I don't feel a burning energy to do this."

Recently, I was offered two big opportunities. Both required that I invest money and time in big proportions. I said to my sweetheart, "I don't feel a burning energy to do this." That was an important point! It's good to listen to yourself.

Now it's your turn. As you talk with people you trust about a particular risk, how do you *really* feel about it? Do you feel a burning energy to do it?

3. If in doubt, leave it out

I've made big decisions. I've led five companies—plus directing my first feature film, giving my first big speech in front of 700 people, writing a book [in a few months my next books will take me up to 50 published books], hiring important team members and more.

Did I have any doubts when I went ahead? I did have a small doubt or two. But during those times, my big, positive burning desire was more important than any fear I had.

On the other hand, a Big, Important Doubt, might be your intuition saying: "Hey! Pay attention to this. Something is OFF here."

If you have that kind of doubt, "leave it out"—that is, protect yourself and don't go down a dark path.

Now it's your turn. Do you have a "Big, Important Doubt"? Is your wish for a particular outcome maybe blinding you to a big downside?

3a. "Bonus": Really wanting it to be true does *not* make it true.

One time, someone invited me to join a business opportunity. When I first heard about the business situation and what *might* blossom out of it, my heart filled up with "Oh! I hope this is true—and this works! My life would change so much. This could be my Big Breakthrough!"

It was necessary for me to quiet down my fantasy-thoughts and take a close look at the whole situation.

I call myself an OptiRealist. That is, I'm optimistic that we can make things better, *and* I'm realistic to know that strategy is necessary. Another realistic view is that any project can get bumpy or even fall apart. Maybe you could barely hold the project together, but with the wrong people involved, you could waste a lot of your time.

For example, I directed a particular film project years ago. A certain actor refused to re-record specific lines of dialogue. This person was afraid of losing close-up shots. Wait a minute! If the scene does not make sense, this actor would still lose!

I carefully explained the need for the scenes to be re-edited to make the whole film project work. Still, this actor refused to record new lines of dialogue.

My solution: I replaced the voice of that actor through the whole film. I had to fix the scenes. That was my job as producer and film director.

A Special Consideration: Realistically *assess if you have enough influence* to make things work.

Ask yourself, "How much control do I have in the project, so I can take action to fix things?" If you have multiple opportunities before you, you may want to focus on those projects that give you a good degree of control, so you *can* fix things.

It is realistic to understand that sometimes people will be so self-focused that they may hurt a project.

My point is: Pay close attention. If you're in a project with trustworthy people, you'll be okay. *If you doubt the professionalism of people involved, it may be time to avoid the deal or situation.*

Now it's your turn. Have you interviewed a lot of people related to the proposed deal or situation? Have you made sure to realize "wanting something to be true does not make it true"?

As an Executive Coach and the Spoken Word Strategist, I often work with clients who need to take appropriate risks. How do you know if the risk is appropriate?

One part of the process is to thoroughly submit the risky deal or situation to these 3 *Considerations Related to Saying "No" to a Particular Risk:*

- "If It's not hell yes, then it's hell no."
- I don't feel a burning energy to do this.
- If in doubt, leave it out.
- Bonus Consideration: Really wanting it to be true does not make it true.

You really need to get access to your intuition. Some researchers identify intuition as *unconscious intelligence.* That is, they suggest that you really *know* something, but it has not risen to the neocortex of the brain yet.

Pay close attention.

Guard your time and resources.

Then you can get the most value when you take an appropriate risk.

More About Making Great Decisions While Facing Risk

(This material was originally shared in my book, *Shape the Future, Lead Like a Pro.*)

My intuition gave me certain questions to help me ascertain if something is what I call the "Right Risk."

- Will I grow?
- Will I learn?
- Will I make new alliances?
- Can I avoid "losing the store"?
- Can I make money all the while?
- Does my heartfelt intuition call me to go forth in this

direction?

Now, I'll talk a bit about each question and add some wise council from Walt Disney.

1) Will I grow? Will I learn?

I've written over 2 million words. Over the years, I have been working to improve in the craft of writing—both nonfiction and fiction. I don't get stuck like I did several years ago. I've learned how to jump in and get writing even when I don't feel like. Writing has become like dancing to me: You stretch, you learn the steps and then you have moments of real grace.

Many of us writers learn to revise and revise.

Get a good idea and stay with it. Dog it, and work at it until it's done right. – Walt Disney

2) Will I make new alliances?

Many times, we make the biggest strides forward when we team up or at least get some coaching. This is one of the reasons why I find so much meaning as the Spoken Word Strategist and Executive Coach. I help my clients learn things faster, get unstuck and streamline their process to reach higher levels of success and fulfillment.

My phrase is: *Alliances make advances.*

In writing 50 books (books #48, #49 and #50 are scheduled to be released in a couple of months), I have learned from working with editors. Often, we go farther faster when we team up with effective people. [As a side note: In high school, I had three extraordinary instructors:

- One taught psychology – I earned a degree in psychology.
- Another emphasized theology – I taught college

level Comparative Religion for over 14 years.

- The third taught advanced literature – I've written screenplays, fiction, non-fiction, songs, and music. I've directed feature films.]

I share the above as evidence that *Alliances make advances.* I am deeply grateful for mentors through the years. I've carried the blessings forward by serving over 5,127 graduate students and college students.

Another example: In the early years, Ub Iwerks drew Mickey Mouse for the first animated Disney films. Without Ub's contribution, Mickey would not have looked nor moved the way he did. This is an example of the power of alliances: Walt Disney's story sense and Ub's design/animation sense.

Later, Ub left the Disney Company to head his own studio. This bothered Walt a lot. Still, it's said that of all the telegrams that arrived to celebrate the success of *Snow White and the Seven Dwarfs,* Walt kept only one telegram—the one from Ub.

Years later, Ub returned to call upon Walt. Ub wanted a job, and Walt gave him the facilities so Ub could experiment with some technical processes. One of Ub's advances made it possible to efficiently make the feature film, *101 Dalmatians.*

Walt had a habit: He would ask the team members to "plus" [add to/improve] each scene of a film.

Now it's your turn.

How can you team up with effective people?

What gaps in your knowledge or resources do you need shored up by working with others?

Write down notes about how you can gain team members or collaborate with others.

3) Can I avoid "losing the store"?

Everyone falls down. Getting back up is how you learn how to walk. – Walt Disney

My point is: Build in a buffer zone so you avoid "losing the store." By this I mean, be careful about a budget and the use of resources. If possible, avoid spending too much on a project.

Some people note that in the same year James Cameron spent $200 million on *Titanic*, Steven Spielberg spent $63 million on *Jurassic Park*.

We realize that *Titanic* called for more expenditures. They built a replica of the great ship, for example.

Still, Steven Spielberg is a master of choosing what to place in a movie and what to leave out.

For example, a river scene with attacking pterodactyls was dropped from *Jurassic Park* (considered too expensive) and only revived for *Jurassic Park III*.

The difference in winning and losing is most often... not quitting. – Walt Disney

To avoid quitting, it can be helpful to retain some money to keep going.

Be careful of budgets of time, money and other resources.

4) Can I make money all the while?
When the Walt Disney Company opens a new theme park they start with a few rides. Then over the years they add more attractions.

Disneyland is like a piece of clay: If there is something I don't

like, I'm not stuck with it. I can reshape and revamp.
 – *Walt Disney*

At the Disneyland Resort, when California Adventure Park opened several things didn't go as planned. In the first year 2001, only 5 million visitors attended. To give perspective to that, in that same year Disneyland saw 12.3 million visitors. In response, the Disney team lowered ticket prices.

How bad were things? The park only had about 5,000 to 9,000 visitors on weekdays although it was built to have a capacity of 33,000.

Okay. That was a rocky start. Disney CEO Bob Iger announced a multi-year revision of the park. It had cost $600 million to build California Adventure Park. The Disney team would further invest $1.1 billion to revise and remodel the park. Let's remember the idea "make money all the while." California Adventure has been open and earning income across the years.

One detail that captures my interest is that the entrance area was changed to a representation of Los Angeles as it appeared when Walt Disney moved there in the 1920s. What a great idea! This brings in the element of magical, nostalgia energy like Disneyland's Main Street U.S.A.

Find ways to bring something to the marketplace and keep improving the product in subsequent versions.

5) Does my heartfelt intuition call me to go forth in this direction?

When you're curious, you find lots of interesting things to do. And one thing it takes to accomplish something is courage.
 – *Walt Disney*

A number of people have asked me, "How did you write over 40 books, Tom?"

I reply, "I was called to each one. I wanted to go on the journey of writing each particular book."

You reach a point where you don't work for money.
— Walt Disney

Walt Disney emphasized: "Disneyland is a work of love. We didn't go into Disneyland just with the idea of making money."

Walt had been called to create Disneyland:

Disneyland really began when my two daughters were very young. Saturday was always 'Daddy's Day' and I would take them to the merry-go-round and sit on a bench eating peanuts, while they rode. And sitting there alone, I felt that something should be built, some kind of family park where parents and children could have fun together. — Walt Disney

So, my friend, I now invite you to pause and ask yourself: "Does my heartfelt intuition call me to go forth in this direction?

My heart has called me to direct feature films, create graphic novels, write and sing songs as part of a band, teach MBA students at Stanford University, write 47 books—and more.

I've answered the call again and again.

What does your heart call you to do?

Yes—there may be years in which you do a "rent job" to support yourself and race home and do your heartfelt work.

We, who adopt the plan of "Whatever it takes," step forward without regrets.

Just imagine what you might do if you quieted down fear and took some good steps forward.

Make a plan and step forward. Shape your future.

Power Principle:

Identify your top considerations that can guard you from taking a misguided risk. Additionally, identify the most important growth-centered considerations that suggest a risk may be worth taking.

Power Questions:

Consider these details if you're considering that a risk is, perhaps, inappropriate:

- "If It's not hell yes, then it's hell no."
- I don't feel a burning energy to do this.
- If in doubt, leave it out.
- Bonus Consideration: Really wanting it to be true does not make it true.

Additionally, consider these questions related to a risk:

- Will I grow?
- Will I learn?
- Will I make new alliances?
- Can I avoid "losing the store"?
- Can I make money all the while?
- Does my heartfelt intuition call me to go forth in this direction?

Tom Marcoux

Create Your Personal Brand—for Success

One powerful process to make you magnetic to many of the best opportunities is to have a powerful, positive personal brand. Such a personal brand gives people a clear idea that you are trustworthy, competent, caring, and worthy of their time and respect. The person with a great personal brand naturally earns more, does more and enjoys more moments of happiness.

A Definition of Personal Brand

The fastest way to think about personal brand is the answer to the question: *What are you best known for?*

A personal brand is more powerful, as a whole process, than just looking at a person's reputation. A reputation may feel like it is simply out of your hands.

Instead, you can apply strategy to forming or enhancing your personal brand.

Recently, I had a pleasant experience related to my personal brand. I talked with a conference organizer who said, "You know, Tom, since you are the Spoken Word Strategist…"

I broke into a big smile. My personal brand was working.

A Moment of Coaching with George Takei

To convince investors that you are a good match for them to fund a project, it helps to come across as coachable. For example, some years ago I was directing my first feature film, and I had a meeting with George Takei (Mr. Sulu—later

Captain Sulu—of *Star Trek*).

I came from directing music videos, so I had storyboards, and I showed him storyboards of this one character. It's 3 o'clock in the morning; the character is really upset. He doesn't know what to do next. A tear rolls down his cheek. The tear goes through the air and lands in his tea cup. It's a slow-motion explosion of tea. A tsunami of tea.

Okay. In a music video, you can get a little esoteric or artsy.

On seeing the storyboard, George Takei said to me, "Uh, Tom. Isn't that a bit melodramatic?"

I agreed with George. And I never filmed the scene. Why? **Because I'm coachable.** Not filming the scene saved time and money. Being coachable is great especially when you're directing your first feature film or doing any new project.

Being coachable makes your personal brand golden.

The Real Power Is in Rehearsal While Being Coached

In my workshop, *Convince Investors to Fund You*, I guide the attendees to break into Teams of Three. They get to rehearse with an instant mini-audience of two attendees in their group.

With clients and audience members, I focus on what I call *Behavior Change through Incremental Evidence*. My idea is that you develop real confidence because you see yourself improving and doing new things—and acting in better ways. That's the positive evidence.

If I see a workshop attendee wringing her hands while delivering part of her pitch, I can guide her in real time to get her hands away from each other. That eliminates one detail that gives the impression of self-doubt.

Another Form of Real Power: Express the Effective Story that Proves You Are Coachable

When you are communicating your personal brand, it's through *story.* So, you don't have to just come out and say, "Hey, I'm coachable."

You can tell an effective story that ends with something like: "That's when my supervisor, George, said, 'Samantha, you're really coachable. You really learned that quickly and you learned how this team works.'"

When interacting with investors, you might find that you will do well to have a story in which *you proved coachable by the results you gained in the marketplace.* For example, having a moniker helps one do well as a public speaker. I have been a professional speaker and member of the National Speakers Association for over 18 years. When I began, I had something generic, "America's Communication Coach."

That was *not* a strong personal brand. It wasn't specific. Some years later, after being in the marketplace and seeing what clients and audiences most resonated with, I gained clarity and expressed my work as the Spoken Word Strategist and Executive Coach.

Once I focused on Spoken Word Strategist, I heard people say "Spoken Word Strategist" in conversations. You know your personal brand is working when you hear it said back to you!

Now it's your turn. What are five words that come up when people talk about you? Pick what *five words would help you* as part of your personal brand.

My advice for an entrepreneur just starting out is to differentiate yourself. Why are you different? What's important about you? Why does the customer need you? – Sara Blakely

(As a side note: I asked my wife, what three words come up when you think of me?" She replied, "Cheerful, determined, annoying." I smiled and said, "I'm cheerfully determined to annoy you.")

Use the S.T.O.R.Y. to Develop Your Personal Brand-Enhancing Story

Using your personal brand is a process of communicating. So, I've developed a system in which I focus on the word S.T.O.R.Y.

S – set how we like the hero
T – target the hero's goal
O – open with a grabber
R – reveal the struggle
Y – yearn for the triumphant ending and
     "What I Learned was…"

1. Set how we like the hero

We like heroes that are *not* arrogant and have some humility. We also appreciate a dash of defiance in our heroes. Such defiance helps make it clear what the hero is opposed to and what the hero is trying to get done.

2. Target the hero's goal

Knowing the hero's goal helps us truly engage with the story. It's vital to have the audience truly understand and feel the hero's goal, so the audience can immediately start rooting for the hero.

3. Open with a Grabber

Imagine this opening to a story:

When Susan came home that night at 10:45 p.m., she closed the front door and heard an unexpected noise in her living room. At that moment her heart raced …

Start the story with something big at stake—the person's life, love relationship, job, something important that is at risk. When I work with a client, I ask questions to find out what is most important to the person. I can ask, "What terrible thing happens if the person does *not* get your product or fails to hire you?"

An interviewer said, "In your example of a story, Tom, you used very visceral terms."

"To create the emotional reaction," I replied. A classic idea is: *people buy on emotion and later justify with facts.*

When I work with a client, we focus on Words – Strategy – Rehearsal. We start with the client's words—that we usually must "dig for." I need to find the client's words in terms of what feels natural coming from their mouth.

Why? Because people can create more energy and more movement in their audience's feelings when they are tuned in with *their* words.

4. Reveal the struggle.
We need to go on the journey. If our main character finds an attacker in her home at 10:45 pm, we get involved as she struggles to survive.

This story could be something that a martial arts school would use to get new students. The struggle engages us. And then we long for a Triumphant Ending.

5. Yearn for the Triumphant Ending and "What I Learned was…"
The Triumphant Ending makes enduring the struggle (with the main character) worth it.

I'll now share a true story that shook me up.

Many years ago, I was at dinner with my then-girlfriend. We visited her friend George and his fiancée Helen, who had invited us to their apartment.

In the middle of dinner, Helen said something that shook me up. Somehow the conversation arrived on self-defense. Helen said, "I know that George can't defend me."

Wow. For many heterosexual male individuals, this is a face-slamming comment.

If I was George, I would have used my smartphone and googled "self-defense" and written down a phone number. Then, I would tell Helen, "Within six days, I will be in a martial arts class."

(In fact, I have taken classes in multiple forms of self-defense, and I practice certain martial art moves every day.)

If I was George, why would have I acted so fast? Because I don't want the person, who is entrusting me with protecting her, to think, "He can't protect me."

My point here is that we have a story that could become a good story that supports a good personal brand. How?

I'll share a fictional version of a story that George could tell:

George: "My point is that I am coachable. In fact, Helen gave me some coaching. One year ago, during a dinner with friends, Helen said, "I know that George can't defend me.' That was really hard coaching to take. But I'm glad she said that. And I'm glad I took action. I said to Helen and our friends, 'Within seven days, I will be in a martial arts class. I took Helen's coaching, and I entered a martials arts class on Day 5. Two weeks later, I switched to another class. I became fit. Helen has seen me spar. She said, 'I'm impressed. I now feel safe with you, George.' And ... as I said, 'I am coachable.'"

When your personal brand is really functioning the way

you want, people will have certain ideas in their mind because they have heard you say it.

For example, I have written and used this phrase: "When you work with me ... you will achieve more than you believe."

I go on to explain that in my work as Spoken Word Strategist and Executive Coach, I am one hundred percent *for* the client. I am all-in. I help the person stretch beyond where they are and transform into a higher level of effectiveness. So, of course, *you will achieve more than you believe.*

To summarize this section, I'll share here the beginning of one of my speeches:

I'm directing my first feature film. I only have a tiny budget, but I do have a contact that gets me—for free—San Luis Obispo Airport and a free use of an American Eagle airplane. How? How can you get the big opportunity?

I'll answer that in two words: Prove it. What I mean by this is that I proved my ability by writing a screenplay for a previous feature film.

That impressed a software engineer who passed the screenplay on to another software engineer, who passed it on to a real estate developer, who passed it on to the then-California Motion Picture Commissioner. He was the person who could get, for my feature film, the San Luis Obispo Airport and an American Eagle airplane. So, I had a big action-filled last scene for my first feature film.

When it comes to Convince Investors to Fund You*—you need to prove it to them. You prove that you are trustworthy with five characteristics—you are confident, competent, connection-building, conflict-skilled and coachable. You develop a powerful* *personal brand.*

Power Principle:

The Real Power is in rehearsal while being coached.

Power Questions:

Have you developed multiple stories that make your personal brand clear? Do you end your story with someone praising you for the virtue that you are emphasizing?

Network for Clients, Contacts and Friends

Networking is an essential part of building wealth.
– Armstrong Williams

Have you noticed that several prosperous people seem at ease in a networking event?

For those of us who are introverts, that can feel like an unreachable summit.

I am an introvert. So, I gained mentors who guided me, and I taught myself many methods to create rapport with new people. Additionally, I shared much of my methods in my prior book, *Relax Your Way Networking.*

Being an introvert is *not* about being shy. It means when you're in a group, *you pay out energy.*

To perform at you best at a networking event ...

- *Rev up* before the event.
- *Recharge* during the event
- *Recover* after the event

If you know you're going to recover after the event, your subconscious mind realizes that you will be okay. You will feel better. That's important.

Here's the Good News: You Can *Recover* Even When Someone Rudely Causes Trouble

Several years ago, I attended a networking event in which I encountered someone who caused a big problem.

I walked into a Chamber of Commerce networking event

and saw a group of four people in conversation and in a circle. I had the intuitive sense that I needed to talk with these people.

A glass of water in my hand, aiming for this group, I walked in the manner of a confident person. I did *not* feel confident, but I decided to adopt the behavior of a confident person.

I walked at a comfortable pace toward them because I didn't want them to think I was coming in fast like a meteor.

Just when I got within earshot, this guy who was talking and holding court, *glared at me and said, "This is a private conversation."*

I felt like the only thing to do was to melt and die. I was so embarrassed. I really felt deflated, shot down, massacred. It really got to me. Can you relate to this?

Some researchers suggest that when we're shot down in a social interaction, our subconscious mind thinks we will not survive. Why? Because in ancient times, those people who were ostracized died due to starvation and exposure.

This guy had been harsh with his glaring and tonality—and "This is a private conversation."

I replied, "That's what I need to know." I turned and strolled away.

Fortunately, my years of training with performance, directing, writing and improvising helped me in that moment of extreme embarrassment.

Still, you now have a method to handle someone disruptive person's put down. Saying, "That's what I need to know" is literally true. It's best to move on to receptive and friendly people.

In my years of meeting thousands of people, this "private conversation" remark only happened once.

However, I know that I have a pre-planned method "in

my pocket" for instant retrieval.

The Power of *Over Prepare*

The number one comment from my clients is: "Tom has helped me become more confident."

I'm glad to hear this. Even better, I'm doing this with a proven system which I summarize as *Words – Strategy – Rehearsal.* I help the person discover his or her best words that feel strong, clear and comfortable as they express it.

Then we apply the clarity of using effective patterns and strategy. Finally, rehearsal creates the transformation. Hence, the person reports becoming more confident. This is based on what I call *Behavior Change through Incremental Evidence.*

I then celebrate the process by saying: *Being prepared for the worst often gets you the best.*

Using the process of Words – Strategy – Rehearsal to give your best performance in networking situations helps you get the tremendous outcomes of excellent networking. These include: getting clients, making contacts, and making alliances—and growing great relationships. That's why I wrote my prior book, *Relax Your Way Networking.* For many of us, networking is stressful. What counts is to think it through and rehearse what questions you might ask. That's part of "over-preparing."

Use A Respectful Way to Close a Difficult Conversation

For many us, it's tough to go to a networking event. You can dead the awkward conversation, in which you just want to escape.

One of my first mentors, Dottie Walters, the grand lady of the speaking industry, taught me a specific technique. I remember her fondly in part due to her kindness and how she helped me leap forward in the speaking industry.

Dottie said that if someone comes across as so egocentric and just keeps talking and talking, you can interrupt them in a skillful, respectful manner.

Some time ago, I had found myself in a conversation that was extreme. I joined a group in which one person *dominated* the conversation. Next thing I know, the other people have left. They've abandoned the conversation.

Now, I wish I had left with the other people. Fortunately, I remembered a method I learned from Dottie. She taught me that one can say, "Oh, that tells me something about you." That gets an egocentric person to pause. They want to know what you have noticed.

Here are examples:

"Oh, that tells me something about you …

- You're so good with details
- You really care a lot about what happens in this industry.
- You are a real leader. I can hear from what you've been telling me—you handled those situations well."

How to Politely End a Conversation

You can say something like: "You know, I promised some people back at the office that I would mingle. So, it's been great talking with you. Have a great evening."

Some clients who might want to use this have said, "But I'm a solopreneur. I don't have people that I must answer to."

Many of us do answer to our spouse or children who visit us in our home office. You promise them that you will do your job properly. You *will* mingle to make great connections and ultimately get more business.

By the way, as you say, "Oh, I promised some people back at the office that I would mingle. So, it's been great talking with you. Have a great evening," you actually step backwards and retreat. That's how you get away!

In my workshops like *Convince Investors to Fund You* and *Pitch with Extreme Confidence,* I have attendees divide into Teams of Three. This means that each person gets an instant mini-audience of two people. Then, the attendees can rehearse.

Rehearsal is crucial to build your real confidence.

* * * * * *

Do not offer your card first. Why? Because it may appear that you're desperate or too pushy.

Unfortunately, some people have a mistaken notion that one "wins" by giving out 20 or 30 business cards.

Not true. Many of those cards will be discarded or lost because you did not have 5 to 10 meaningful conversations. The business card means something when the person has enjoyed talking with you.

For a networking event, I'll give myself a goal like I want to have five great conversations. And I'm going to share contact information with four people. Recently, I was at a conference for four hours and I had conversations with 24 people.

At a previous conference, I attended about three hours a day on three days, I gained the contact information of 65 people. How was that possible? At that conference, these attendees specialized in the helping professions (coaches, healers and more). I began conversations with, "How do you help people?" The people enjoyed talking about their work and how they felt about it.

It's more important for you to get their contact information. You can say, "It has been really great talking with you. It would be good to stay in contact, so do you have a card?"

Surprisingly, many of us discover that about 73% of the people do not have a handy business card. What? It *is* a networking event.

No problem. You say, "That's okay. I'll make you one," and you pull out a 3 x 5 card from your pocket and you write down their information. I ask, "Are you at Gmail?" Why? I don't want to be intrusive.

The person may have an email address that they use for specific interactions. But usually they just give me their business email address. They're comfortable, and sometimes people say, "Let me give you my phone number, too."

Many times, it's easier to avoid the awkwardness of some possible romantic notion by just asking for an email address.

What counts is that you get *their* contact information. It does not matter as much to give them your business card. Why? They lose it or toss it in a drawer with the other 27 business cards they received at that networking event.

Several of my clients decide to "do their homework" by sending an email to each person they met before they go to sleep that same night.

You avoid losing track of the person. You don't have to worry about their business card.

Still, I often group the business cards by the event. (Later, I separate the material into other categories in my filing system.)

Use *The Wrap-It Method* to Capture Notes

Avoid writing on the person's business card, particularly if you're working with Asian individuals. Why? Because the business card itself is representing their company. So, writing on the business card is like writing on that person's face.

Instead, I use a method I call *The Wrap-It Method.* I take notes on a sheet in a pocket-sized memo book. Then I rip the page out and wrap it around the person's business card. I place the now-wrapped card in my pocket.

Later, I send a follow-up email and reference the tip that person shared with me. Some people express their surprise about how I remembered their comment.

How to Help Someone Feel Good While They Talk with You

When appropriate you can ask, "What are you looking forward to?" The person might ask, "What do you mean? In business or a vacation?"

You reply, "Whatever you prefer to talk about."

If they start talking about a business detail, it's great. If they start talking about a vacation, it's even better.

Another question I may ask is, "I'm curious. What's one of your hobbies—something you do to relax?" This is how we get people talking about what they like and enjoy talking about.

With my clients, I focus on *Words – Strategy – Rehearsal.* I have my clients rehearse what they'll ask at a conference. In these rehearsals, I improvise and portray various people the client might engage in a conversation. This process helps them *over prepare.*

I emphasize that one does well to ask *gentle questions*—the ones which are easy and sometimes fun to answer.

This is *not* about impressing the other person. Instead,

you help the person have a great time because you're a great listener.

Power Principle:

You are genuine and comfortable at a networking event by planning and rehearsing your questions before you arrive at the event.

Power Questions:

Have you identified the ways you will close an awkward conversation? Have you rehearsed your conversation-closes? Have you identified gentle questions you can ask to start conversations?

Warm Up Relationships with Humor (How to Be Funny)

Repeat anything often enough and it will start to become you.
– Tom Hopkins

Imagine you could warm up your relationships and create a real connection. In this section, I'm sharing how to warm up your business relationships, personal relationships—and even warm up your relationship with an audience.

The skillful use of humor can help you warm up a relationship. What's the safest way to introduce humor?

The quick answer is: When you use humor that is against yourself. Still, you even need to be careful here. If you use humor about being disorganized, you destroy your chance of landing either a job or a significant client.

The idea is to use humor that shows you as human—and that you do *not* take yourself too seriously.

For example, often when I start one my workshops, I begin with a brief story:

I'm at Sun Microsystems, and I'm speaking for 20 minutes in front of the audience when suddenly, from the back of the room, my assistant waves and gestures: "Zip up your fly! Zip up your fly!"

So, I nod to her so that she stops waving frantically. Then I say to the audience, "I've just been given some important information. I'll be right back."

I step off the stage and exit out a backdoor. I zip up and return through that door. I say to the audience, "For those of you who know what just happened ... okay. For those of you who don't know what just happened ... good!"

I turned this form of disaster into one of the biggest laughter moments I've created for an audience.

A little bit of self-deprecating humor can do much for your connection with the audience.

My error with my pants zipper did not evaporate my expertise related to *Pitch with Extreme Confidence.*

But this situation shows that I have a sense of humor about myself. I just acknowledged my humanness.

A bit of humor directed at yourself works. We realize that humor—and all humor has a target—directed at someone else or some group can create an *immediate disconnect* with your audience.

Avoid Telling a Joke at the Beginning of Your Speech

Some people can tell jokes and some people can't. And, some of us can learn to do something effective—tell a story that has a bit of humor mixed in.

Avoid telling a joke at the beginning of your pitch or speech. Why? You could lose 75% of your audience in just a couple of seconds.

So, unless your name is Ellen DeGeneres, don't open a speech with humor.

Instead, seek to make a real connection. For example, recently, I opened with: "How many of us here in this room want to convince investors to fund us?

Most of the Time, Use Yourself as the Target of Your Humor

You never know who is in your audience. Furthermore, people tend to record things with their smartphone. Anything you say could be recorded and placed in social media—instant scandal. Avoid this!

As a professional speaker, I follow the advice of one of my mentors. He said, "You may talk with someone who uses curse words, but he may not like hearing them come out of your mouth."

In my personal life, I just avoid curse words. This served me well when I almost fell off a stage while giving a speech. I said, "Oh! That was exciting."

If I habitually cursed in my personal life, my reaction would have been ... well, you know.

I have noted, with my MBA students, that I don't swear in a public setting because that practice makes it easier to be invited back to certain venues.

Our habits that we have in our regular life can bleed over into our stage life.

How to Know When You're Doing Something with Too Much Self-Deprecation

Be careful to avoid beating yourself up in front of an audience.

It's vital to notice the difference between the trouble of calling yourself "stupid" in certain areas — or just observing lightly those little human quirks we all tend to have.

For example, I didn't lose my IQ points when I had a difficulty with my zipper being down. I've coined a phrase: "I was the clown with the zipper down."

The point is: Share your amusement about your humanness. And, avoid twisting your humor into some kind of weird therapy in front of an audience. (This material above is for the people who give an occasional speech. On the other hand, stand-up comedians have a completely different set of guidelines.)

How to Recover If You Mix Up Your Words

It helps to memorize these words: "Oh, that's not what I meant to say. What I meant to say was ..." Then you immediately correct your error.

You'll Do Well with Humor When You Practice Your "Recovery Lines"

For over 18 years, I've been a professional member of the National Speakers Association, and I've noticed that we, speakers, find some bits of humor do not land with every crowd. For example, some years ago, I gave a speech to 237 people at DeAnza College in California. To illustrate something about stress, I used a metaphor related to *Star Trek*.

I went into a William Shatner (Captain Kirk) overacting tone and said, "Spock! Raise the ... stress shields."

I got a couple of chuckles.

I *recovered* with, "I guess that one was for the Trekkies."

I got some laughter. That was better.

(I call myself a *Star Trek* enthusiast. So, I'm aware that the correct term is "Trekker.")

My point here is that it's good to preplan some "Recovery Lines."

In giving a speech, your plan is to look poised and confident. An important part of this process is to gracefully use Recovery Lines. Here's an example: "I think that line was for my mom" — which acknowledges that a bit of humor was not successful in the room with this audience.

Since you look unfazed by one bit of humor failing, the audience continues to feel comfortable with you.

Be Ready for the Awkward Silence-Moment

Already I shared how I worked the moment when I didn't get much of a response and I said, "I guess that one was for the Trekkies."

Another situation when the Awkward Silence-Moment arises is when you ask for questions during a speech. If no one offers a question, you can say, "Oh, this is good. People are thinking."

If you don't look flustered, the audience feels comfortable. Why? Because *you* look comfortable. You do not look bothered by the silence.

For example, I was giving a speech at IBM when I got stuck. I did not know what my next two sentences would be. So, I said, "I need to pause for a moment. My brain needs more RAM."

At IBM, the audience found that to be hilarious. A Random-Access Memory joke.

Tell A Story with Humor in It—Rather than Telling a Joke

Some of us are just not good at telling jokes. Here's a solution: Tell a story that has a humorous element to it.

For example, here is a classic story told over the years from Red Skelton to an episode of the TV Show *The West Wing*:

It's a big flood, and a gentleman climbs to his balcony and the water comes up to his waist.

A boat comes along, and the person says, "Get in the boat. We'll save you."

The guy says, "No, the Lord will save me."

"All right." And the boat continues onward.

Now the water keeps on coming. He climbs up to his roof. The water is up to his knees.

Another boat comes along. "Get in the boat. We'll save you."

"No, the Lord will save me."

The person in the boat shakes her head and moves on.

Soon, the water is up to the guy's neck. He looks up and finds a helicopter hovering overhead. "Grab the rope. We'll save you."

"No. The Lord will save me."

"Idiot," says the pilot.

The helicopter goes away. The water keeps coming, and he goes and sees the Lord.

He gets to the Pearly Gates. He asks, "Lord, why didn't you save me?"

And the Lord scratches his head and says, "I don't understand this. I mean, I sent you two boats and a helicopter."

When I tell this story, I add a helicopter sound by tapping my palm on my chest as I say "Grab the rope. We'll save you." This simulates the thumping sound of the helicopter blades.

I shared the above story because, even if you don't get the laugh, you can say something like: "My point with this story is we need to be alert to who can help us. And that's it okay to get help. Where is a boat or helicopter coming to help *you* —in your life?"

An Introvert Has an Advantage Related to Humor

The introvert likes to think things through so he or she can refine the words of a humor bit.

Recently, I worked on a bit of humor: We have in the neighborhood a cat named Baxter. He's always running away. I don't know if he has a front, so I call him Butt Baxter.

For cat enthusiasts, this detail may elicit a smile. They are quite familiar with timid cats.

We know that people like cats, but if you have a cat joke you better have a dog joke. For example, I say, "There's an inverse relationship about dogs. The smaller the dog, the bigger the mouth."

These are small bits of humor. Whether they work or not with a particular audience depends on the context.

Practice with a Safe Audience

We want to make sure that we have a good, supportive practice audience. We want someone who is rooting for us. This person must be someone with whom we feel safe to experiment. It takes some efforts and false starts to find your material that works.

Professional comedians practice new humor in small venues. Stand-up comic George Carlin would work all year, trying his material in small venues, and then at the end of the year he would record an HBO special. He did that 14 times.

To Use Humor, Have Preplanned Ways to Recover When the Humor Bit Fails

Standup comedian Eddie Izzard uses one of my favorite methods. When a bit of humor does not work with an audience, Eddie pantomimes writing on a tablet in his hand. He says, "Never connect those two things again."

The audience laughs.

Why? The laughter moment arises out of the recognition that some things just don't work. And we feel a warm connection with the comedian. Eddie looks like he has just learned something.

Humor is helpful in showing how you avoid taking yourself too seriously. For example, I'm not trying to fulfill a fictional image of being some sort of guru.

Recently, I was working with a client, Angela. I asked, "What do you want your persona to be? Do you want to come across as *the* expert—someone who has solved a problem, and everything is great for you? Or do you want to, on your blog, show some vulnerability and show that you're in the middle of things, and you're facing similar problems that your readers face?"

"Which is better?" Angela asked.

"It's up to you. It depends on *your* intuition," I began. "It's easier to present yourself as a human being, a facilitator, a coach. And to *avoid* trying to come across as a guru— someone who is never gets upset or never has an off moment or never has a bit of humor that doesn't work."

Angela chose to express herself as a person who *works with* the issues that she shares with her audience.

You've probably noticed that several people are looking to identify "false icons" (ones who put on a face of "I'm more peaceful than you"). Some critics revel when a "false icon" falters and reveals that they're not as enlightened or "put together" as they pretend to be.

The good news is: When you show that you can take a light approach to your own humanness, the audience joins with you. "Hey, you're one of us—imperfect human beings."

Power Principle:

You can do better with humor when you preplan your Recovery Lines for when a bit of humor may fail.

Power Questions:

Have you identified some Recovery Lines you can use in case a bit of humor fails? Have your rehearsed with safe audiences?

How to Use Your Intuition Well

Don't let the noise of others' opinions drown out your own inner voice. And most important, have the courage to follow your heart and intuition. – Steve Jobs

Following my intuition, I have made decisions that have yielded income every month for years. Some of these decisions are about books I've written that generate monthly income.*

* For more about this topic, see my book, *The Writer's Solution —Crush Your Self-Doubt.*

My co-host Johanna on our podcast *Introverts Own Your Voice*, spoke of how her intuition helped her save her own life.

Here's how Johanna described the situation:

"Some years ago, I got into my car after going to school one day. I drove up to a light. It turned green. Normally, I would just go right away, but something held me back. Inside, something said, Not yet. *I waited there feeling kind of foolish for a few seconds, and then a car went racing through the intersection. If I had turned when I was going to turn, I would have been killed."*

If Johanna had not listened to her intuition, she would help been crushed by the speeding car. That vehicle would have smashed into her driver's side door.

Intuition is always right in at least two important ways; It is always in response to something. It always has your best interest at heart. – Gavin De Becker

The above ideas from Gavin De Becker are useful in that many of us wonder what "voice" inside we're listening to. Is it intuition or fear?

Don't try to comprehend with your mind. Your minds are very limited. Use your intuition. — Madeleine L'Engle

You must train your intuition—you must trust the small voice inside you which tells you exactly what to say, what to decide.
– Ingrid Bergman

In this section, we will look at various facets of how to use your intuition well. One important point is that it often helps to slow down so you can hear the voice of intuition.

Intuition will tell the thinking mind where to look next.
– Jonas Salk

What is one's intuition?

Intuition is knowing, but *not* only using your rational thinking. You know something on a feeling level.

Gerd Gigerenzer, as a researcher and scientist, looks at intuition as *data that hasn't risen to the conscious level yet.*

It's powerful to pay attention to how you feel (perhaps, "in your gut") about something. You may not be able to put your reasons into words. Still, you can make the right call.

Introverts have an advantage in that we're good at thinking things through. Such a process often gives an introvert an edge in many situations.

Let's return to Gavin de Becker's comment:

Intuition is always right in at least two important ways. It is always in response to something. It always has your best interest at heart. – Gavin de Becker

Gavin de Becker pointed out that we can naturally protect ourselves if we would avoid distracting ourselves from our gut feelings. For example, some people see an elevator car arriving on their floor and see someone in that elevator car. These individuals instantly get a bad feeling about the situation. But instead of listening to their feeling, they think "Oh, this is silly" or "Someone might see me refuse to get on the elevator car and think that I'm stupid or paranoid."

In speeches I continue the story by saying: "We have a word for those people ... *dead*."

The advice from author Gavin de Becker is that we listen to our intuition!

Here is another distinction to consider:

Voice of Fear: contract, hide, do not take an appropriate risk

Voice of Intuition: expand, experiment, take an appropriate risk

How Do You Make Better Use of Your Intuition?

First, you need to make space for your intuition. This means that you plan things out, so you can have time to hear your intuition. This can be a simple plan to "sleep on it" and see what insights and feelings you have the next morning.

You can devote six minutes or up to 15 minutes for a simple form of meditation. You just focus on your breath going in and out. One time during such a meditation a great idea arose in my thoughts for a client. I wrote the idea down.

Perhaps, you would enjoy taking a walk and getting fresh air as your way to make space for your intuition.

For some people, sharing a new idea does *not* work because the new idea is too "fragile" and subject to the naysayers.

I have been fortunate in that I can hear opposing viewpoints to my idea, and I observe if the idea becomes stronger in my *own* feelings.

For example, years ago, I attended a seminar in which the leader was doing manipulative actions toward my friends. This bothered me. The next day, I wrote 2,000 words in the professor's lounge just before I taught graduate students. My writing became the seed for a book. And my intuition served up a title: *Darkest Secrets of Persuasion and Seduction Masters: How to Protect Yourself and Turn the Power to Good.*

Unfortunately, a number of people around me said, "Oh, no, don't use that title. I don't like it. It sounds too in-your-face, too splashy. It sounds like a gimmick. Don't do that."

Instead, I'm glad that I followed my own intuition. That book has sold every month—for years.

Following my intuition has worked well for me. These following books sell every month:

- *Darkest Secrets of Film Directing*
- *Darkest Secrets of Making a Pitch to the Television and Film Industry*
- *Darkest Secrets of Charisma*

I've found that my intuition acts like a friend. I get some guidance, and I take action. And, the situation flows as if my intuition says, "Oh, you act on my advice, Then, I will give you more valuable advice."

Find You Own Way to Solve Problems and Follow Your Own Intuition

Sometimes, when other people are clamoring for you to avoid going with your gut feelings, you can find that things become clearer for you. Still, realize that you may not be able to (so far) vocalize what your reasoning is for your course of action. Why? Your intuition is operating on a level that is not framed by logic and rational arguments. Your personal truth can exist on the gut feelings level. This means that if you don't feel you can justify what you want to do with a wonderful argument based on logic, *stop*. That is, avoid entering a conversation in which you find yourself just making up reasons.

People around you will shoot down these flimsy reasons—because they are *not* based on what you know subconsciously.

Beware that You Might Have a Habitual Way of Approaching Life that Is Holding You Down

For example, I know someone who seems determined that everyone in a room knows that he is the smartest one there and that he has all the answers—and that he has thought of everything first.

One day, during a break during one of my workshops, I privately said to this person: "If you're always the sharpest, most intelligent person in the room, you're in the wrong room."

In that conversation, I meant that this person was relying only on *his* counsel, *his* thinking, and *his* rational thought. He was not making space for other people's intuition. He also had no space for other people's thoughts or different perceptions built on their unique life experiences. This problem creates the "lone hotshot" who, like any human being, can miss things.

Here's another potential problem for an introvert. I call it the *All-or-nothing Problem.* Since introverts pay out energy, we may notice that we're saying *no* to several opportunities. Then we get mad at ourselves and feel shame that we're not going to enough networking events or chances to give a speech. We may refuse to attend gatherings or parties.

The solution to the All-or-nothing Problem is to become truly selective. Pick the best networking event for the month. Reserve your energy for that one event.

I've often said that if an extravert has a giant pizza pie of energy, then an introvert has a pecan pie of energy. If you only have these slices of pecan pie, you need to be selective in what events you attend. Pick the best. So, it is not about avoiding all events. You just make sure to reserve your energy for the select few events that will do you the most good. You're going to need to, on purpose, rev up before a networking event or even before going to some form of entertainment (a movie, play, concert, ballet, or something else). The idea is that for you to be awake and alive for the event, you need to guard your energy before the event. I call it rev up. For example, before seeing a play in the evening, see if you can *avoid* scheduling an afternoon group meeting prior to your evening's entertainment.

In summary, be sure you make space, so you can connect with your gut feelings—your intuition. Use this path to making better decisions.

Power Principle:
Make space for your intuition. Take some time and

discover what gut feeling may arise to guide your decisions.

Power Questions:

Where do you feel an intuitive "nudge" in your body? (in your abdomen, your shoulders, your chest—somewhere else?) When has intuition worked for you? How did the process go for you?

Tom Marcoux

Use Leverage for Wealth

To be celebrated, to be wealthy, to have power requires access to major institutions. – C. Wright Mills

Wealth is built through leverage, and in many different ways. The rich are masters at leveraging their contacts, credibility, money, education, other people's money, and just about anything else you can think of to create large results with little effort. ... Just get on the inside. – Steve Siebold

Leverage is a powerful idea. However, many individuals shy away from leverage, perhaps, because they equate it with manipulation. Instead, I have learned that **the proper and powerful use of leverage is all about relationships and trust.**

Above, I shared the quote that includes "power requires access to major institutions." That's all about building relationships enhanced by trust.

Some years ago, I wanted to break into the film industry. I wanted to do a feature film, and I had no contacts at all. In my life, I have broken into a number of industries, including the speaking industry, the film industry and academia. With no contacts.

I learned to develop business relationships and even friendships when starting with a cold beginning—no contacts.

As I mentioned, some years ago, I wanted to get into the film industry. One way to break in is to write a screenplay. It becomes your calling card. My screenplay goes from one software engineer to another software engineer to a real estate developer and finally to the then-California Motion Picture Commissioner. Later, when I'm directing a different feature film, he lets me know that he can get—for free—the San Luis Obispo Airport and an American Eagle plane for my film production.

I replied, "This is fantastic. I don't have a place for that in the screenplay yet, but I'll get back to you in a day or two. And I will find a place to put that location and plane into the screenplay."

So, I wrote and filmed a scene utilizing both the airport and airplane, which became the *big finish* for my first feature film that I directed. I also produced and acted in this feature film that went to the Cannes film market.

As you can see, I went into action immediately to accept this big opportunity offered by an elder in the film industry. Because this man was impressed with my screenwriting, he trusted me. And I had a form of leverage.

I only had a chance to have this opportunity because I had a good relationship. I had a mentor, and I had leverage. This is the essence of what we're talking about with *use leverage for wealth.*

Recently, an interviewer asked me, "How do you get past the impression that leverage is manipulation?"

I replied, "First, we have to pause to see if it is literally manipulation."

Here is an old comment:

Give me a lever long enough and a fulcrum on which to place it, and I shall move the world. – Archimedes

So, leverage is *not* manipulation. Leverage is about movement. Leverage is about power, but *it is truly about* *influence.* When I have taught MBA students about the difference between manipulation and persuasion, I made it visual. I used pantomime—as if I have a something in my hand "manipulation," and I tossed it down on the floor, and I stepped on "this horrible manipulation."

Then I pantomimed holding "persuasion" above my head as if it was bathed in a golden shaft of heavenly light. **Persuasion is about serving the other person you're talking with.**

Instead, **manipulation is pulling strings on someone, and the manipulator does *not* care about the other person's well-being.** If someone sells you a product that does you no good or harms you, that is manipulation.

Instead, **if someone provides a service or product that enhances your life, that is *persuasion*.** Because what you are doing is connecting with what they need, what they want, and where they want to go. The person says, "Of course, I want your product. I want your service."

We are developing a business relationship.

You've probably noted that people like to feel good. When you do well and develop a relationship with someone who is an elder in an industry, they will enjoy helping you. As I mentioned the California Motion Picture Commissioner helped me to have the San Luis Obispo Airport and an American Eagle plane. He liked me, and he trusted me to do good work. I imagine that he enjoyed helping a rising person in the industry. Maybe, he saw a bit of himself in me.

At the time I knew him, he was older, having acted in a feature film opposite Cary Grant.

He was not acting much. *Because I knew he would enjoy it,* I wrote a role for him in my feature film. In the closing scene of my feature film, he portrayed the manager of the airport. My character named "Son," runs through his airport.

The manager says, "Whoa, son."

"How do you know my name?" my character responds.

A comedic moment in the film—that I wrote as a change in the script the night before we actually filmed it.

It's wonderful and a joy to be the writer and director of a project. You can change things—creating some excitement and fun—and still express what you wanted originally to emphasize in your screenplay.

That's the reason that several feature film score composers also serve as conductors of their own music.

So, my point is: It's valuable for us to get past that perception that leverage means manipulation. **Leverage means movement.** To move a boulder, you place the lever and the fulcrum in the right places, and you can press down lightly on the lever with your hand. Then you have the power of ten power weightlifters. That's when you use leverage. Now, I will share ideas embodied in the word LIFT. If you want to be a prosperous person, with a lot of positive impact on the world, you need to rise. That's the reason we use the L.I.F.T. process:

L – lead yourself

I – inspire

F – focus

T – trim

1. Lead yourself

You can only become truly accomplished at something you love. Don't make money your goal. Instead, pursue the things you love doing, and then do them so well that people can't take their eyes off you. – Maya Angelou

Be so good they can't ignore you. – Steve Martin

Courage is doing something despite the fear, and I've worked hard on being a courageous person. – Sara Blakely

You need to be *charged up* in your thoughts. To be prosperous, you need to get out of the limited thinking patterns that hold that one must hurt people to go forward. In fact, the people who do quite well are great at building relationships. Creating trust. This means so much to me that in a little while from now, I'm going to have the 20th anniversary edition of my book, *Be Heard and Be Trusted.*

So, the idea is to lead yourself so that you can implement *be heard and be trusted.*

I must lead myself to protect my own energy. For example, sometimes, I avoid seeing certain feature films at the movie theater. I tell family members that some films will take away my energy. That would cripple my efforts to get positive things done.

I prefer to feel better after I see a feature film, on my way out of the movie theater. I want to feel stronger after an experience. I don't want to tear myself apart and slow myself down.

To develop your prosperity, you need to lead yourself.

*Most of the reason we don't do things is because we're afraid to fail. I just made a decision one day that I was **not** not going to do things in my life because of fear. – Sara Blakely*

2. Inspire

You inspire people to join you in a cause to fulfill a vision. This is when we start to hear things like OPM—other people's money. I also say that OPM means learning from *other people's mistakes.* If you study and learn, then you can save time, money and other resources.

That's why I get excited about my episodes of *Introverts Own Your Voice* (the podcast on iTunes—with videos on youtube.com). In several episodes, I also share mistakes and what I learned from them, so you don't have to make such mistakes. This saves you time, money and resources.

Now it's your turn. Look at these possibilities. How can you create positive leverage with these elements?

- OPI – other people's ideas
- OPT – other people's thoughts
- OPE – other people's efforts
- OPL – other people's labor
- OPC – other people's capital—in terms of investment in what you're doing

Leverage is all about building relationships and building trust.

3. Focus

The successful warrior is the average man, with laser-like focus.
– Bruce Lee

With my clients and audiences, I emphasize what I call **The Power of Three.** We need to make a conscious choice to avoid falling prey to every single invite we get to join so many emerging social media modalities. It can be much more powerful to focus on specific social media modalities like LinkedIn. You avoid the mistake of being scattered and spreading your time and efforts too thin across too many social media modalities.

Focusing can also help you quiet down the voice of fear. Focus and take action. I often say: *When you're in action you're focused, and fear is a quiet voice in the background.*

4. Trim

People think focus means saying yes to the thing you've got to focus on. But that's not what it means at all. It means saying no to the hundred other good ideas that there are. You have to pick carefully. I'm actually as proud of the things we haven't done as the things I have done. Innovation is saying no to 1,000 things.
– Steve Jobs

Trim is a vital part of the coaching programs that I offer to clients.

For example, I have A.C.T. coaching: *Assess, Create, and Trim.*

Trim helps you avoid the mistake of attempting to keep cramming more and more activity into your days.

Many of us have heard about working smarter and not harder. Trimming helps us indeed work smarter. It also gives us the space to put in your required recovery time.

Working smarter is about being decisive. That includes choosing carefully what to cut from your schedule.

For example, I watch a certain amount of television and only certain films because I am involved in the creation of media franchises. One of my favorite projects is about a character named Jenalee Storm, who is 17 years old, in her first year of college—and she deals with magic and dragons.

In the Hollywood industry I have a couple of people who keep me posted about certain details that are going on in the industry.

Still, I watch certain TV shows and feature films to keep my attention on the pulse of the media.

I still focus on *trim* to optimize my productivity. I trim certain TV shows out of my daily habits. I stop watching a show if it becomes too predictable or it does not fully engage me. I also cut TV shows from my viewing schedule if they will not help me improve in the kind of writing that I do.

Identify Naysayers and Reduce Your Exposure to Them (Trim what drains your life)

Unfortunately, some people (perhaps, certain friends and family members), function as Naysayers in your life.

Earlier, I mentioned a metaphor: some people act like crabs. If crabs are in a bucket, and one heroic crab tries to escape, the other crabs will pull the individual down. They will not allow that crab to leave.

Naysayers do not want you to leave them behind. They'll fill your ears with "mud." These are Dark Memes.

A meme is "an element of a culture or system of behavior" passed from person to person. Sure, we're inundated with images on Facebook. Some are funny. However, some "common sense" ideas are like leeches that take away ambition, vision and personal energy.

At the beginning of this book, I mentioned "Well-Intentioned Saboteurs." They may not have malevolent intent toward you, but they still say things that are like pollution. These Saboteurs merely repeat Dark Memes.

Examples of Dark Memes:
- Don't Get Rich, Live Rich.
- Money is the root of all evil.
- Rich people have no compassion.
- Behind every fortune is a crime.

Study the most successful self-made millionaires, and you'll find a substantial trail of satisfied customers. – Steve Siebold

Notice a true difference between a naysayer and a coach who has real experience in the area in which you want to

become extraordinary.

Naysayer	Coach (who has experience)
You've never been good at talking in front of people.	Speaking in front of a group is a learnable skill. We'll make sure that you rehearse well. We'll use strategies, and we'll find your unique ways to excel.
You know how few people make money by writing?	You can find a genre in which they are a significant number of readers. When you apply your efforts and pay close attention, you *can* improve your writing. We'll pay close attention to *your unique voice.* You will develop an audience—your Tribe.

The coach gives constructive feedback as opposed to how a naysayer vomits destructive nonsense that tears down one's subconscious mind.

Reduce your exposure to the naysayer. You don't cut off a family member completely, but you do reduce your exposure.

* * * * * *

I serve as the Spoken Word Strategist and Executive Coach for my clients. I also have my own coach and mentors. To perform at your best, you need people you trust to point out your gaps and help you. You can improve skills—for example improving one's listening skills pays big dividends of creating relationships built on trust. Otherwise, your coach may advise that you hire certain team members or contractors to cover your gaps.

The smartest thing I ever did was to hire my weakness.
– Sara Blakely

Special Situation: How does an introvert fail to develop leverage for wealth?

The difficulty is that when an introvert participates in a meeting, gives a speech or simple talks on the phone, he or she actually *pays out* energy. The introvert easily feels depleted.

Here's another tough situation. A significant number of us introverts can feel like we've lost our energy by just thinking of an upcoming meeting. It is like anticipating being drained of blood *before* you get to the blood lab.

This pre-event experience of feeling drained often prods an introvert to hide or isolate the self. That's when opportunities to develop leverage for wealth are missed.

Beware of these Ways to Fail with Leverage:
- Fail to take care of your relationships
- Don't go and connect with new people at networking events.
- Fail to jump at a great opportunity to give a speech and make new connections, new allies and new clients.

In earlier years, I found myself confronted with a truly big problem about having enough energy to attend several networking events and to give a number of speeches. Even phone calls require significant energy, but they're crucial to develop business relationships.

I learned that I had to take better care of my own personal energy. Then I would have the energy to make the new contacts necessary to get big things done. I deeply want to manifest certain things. For example, I'd like my novel series *Jenalee Storm* to land with multiple episodes through some media modality (Perhaps, *Jenalee Storm* will land on Netflix or another option). To make this happen I need to meet new people. Additionally, I need to take care of the people I already know.

It's amazing how often I get emails or Facebook chats from people who say, "I'm no good at staying in touch with people. Tom, you are so good about staying current and checking in with me and seeing how I'm doing."

The truth is: **Anyone who fails to develop the ability to take good care of relationships is basically affirming that they want to stay stuck.** Now, that seems strange. Who would want to be stuck? It's a situation that is created *by default*. Here's analogous example. Recently. I met a couple of elderly people, who refused to get out daily and take a walk. There's no big surprise that some of them are losing the ability to walk at all. That is a bad situation caused by falling into a default, disempowering complacency.

Beware of the Big Mistake in Failing to Develop Leverage

The big mistake is failing to take care of your relationships. For example, an introvert must become skilled to take care of his or her personal energy. Why? It's important to have the energy so that you *check in* with people and see how they're doing *before* you need them. Be kind and helpful as your way of life—and as a natural way of creating warm relationships.

In my book, *Relax Your Way Networking*, I emphasize

There are 3 R's: Rev Up, Recharge and Recover.

In the middle of a networking event, *Recharge* is about getting off the stage. Get away from other people. Go to a restroom stall and catch your breath. Perhaps, you might read a couple paragraphs of an empowering book on your smartphone.

During a conference, I'll say to my sweetheart, "Let's go take a walk. Let's get away from all the noise."

Then I feel recharged and give her hug, just before I return to the conference for a session when attendees mingle.

I'm almost like a soldier, who needs to go back onto the field or like a gladiator who needs to return to the arena.

To develop Leverage for Wealth and to create prosperity, you must be in the arena. Additionally, you need to take care of the people that you know.

Leverage requires relationships built on trust.

So, you can't develop trust if you don't have the energy to be fully present with a person. You need to listen to this person.

Introverts find that they need to recharge their energy before they appear in public. An introvert can make the mistake of isolating the self too much. It almost becomes a habit.

The counter to the isolation-habit is to consciously choose to have some time in your daily schedule to recharge. For example, each day I have at least one hour when I'm away from everyone. That's when I'm probably listening to music and assembling a jigsaw puzzle.

In summary …
L stand for Lead Yourself.
It all begins with how skillful you are with leading

yourself. Do you do what's necessary to guard your energy, so you can perform at your best?

I stands for Inspire.

Here's a valuable example of *inspiring* your team members.

Recently, I was working with a team member who endured some tough family times. The person completed a phase of a project, but it was a bit late.

My intention as a leader is to meet our deadlines and make sure that team members stay focused, positive and productive. Strategically, I decided to have *two* meetings.

The first conversation included my expressing appreciation for what the team member had accomplished. I celebrated the good work.

Soon after, I scheduled a second meeting that focused on discovering methods so that my team member would be more adept at staying on schedule.

You need to inspire people by thanking them and expressing appreciation—and celebrating what good work is accomplished.

In a separate meeting, you provide guidance or constructive feedback. Be sure to avoid trying to cram everything together. Remember that people only remember about three things of any meeting or any speech.

T stands for Trim

For you to have the energy to create prosperity, whether you are an introvert or not, you must *Trim down your schedule*. It does not work to keep on cramming more and more in. You must be selective.

For example, I helped a client, Parker, who was giving away too much time to people who did not hire him.

We worked out a phrase for him to say: "This is about the time when my wife says, 'Is that a client? Don't give away the store.'"

This was a unique solution for my client, Parker.

Still, this helped him Trim his schedule, and in some cases shift someone into one of his coaching programs.

Remember, to develop Leverage for Wealth, streamline your work life and trim your own schedule. Be sure to have enough recovery time so you can perform at your best when it's necessary.

Power Principle:

The proper and powerful use of leverage is all about relationships and trust.

Power Questions:

How are you devoting enough time, attention and effort to building your relationships, so people trust you (and you develop leverage)? Are you trimming your schedule, so you guard your personal energy and can take better care of your relationships?

Convince Investors to Fund You: Master the 3 Critical Factors of Pitch, Network and Follow-Up

At certain conferences, after I have served as a Pitch Judge, people leading startup companies come up to me. I'm glad to be helpful. Some of them come on too strong, and it's clear no one trained them in how to create rapport before they make "the big ask." A realization blossomed in my thoughts: *Investors know on a subconscious mind level that some startup leaders are pros and others are amateurs.*

I trust that you've seen that first impressions sometimes cannot be transformed, so it is crucial to do your best to prepare. You need to make the excellent impression on someone who can change your life for the better.

The big idea here is that certain individuals may know how to pitch but crash and burn when it comes to networking and follow-up.

You need to know how to respond if an investor comes up and says, "I'd like to know more about what you're doing."

The truth is that the entrepreneurial idea is not always king or queen. It's whether you are trustworthy. Basically, an investor says, "Yes, I want to go on this adventure with you."

The problem about an adventure is that somewhere along the line you can get hit and bleed.

The investor is saying, "Can I trust you to lead?"

Two Major Ideas Related to Convincing Investors

To convince investors to fund you, hone your skills related to…

• Be heard and be trusted.*

• Investors are testing you all along the way.

* In a short time, I will be releasing the 20th Anniversary edition of my book, *Be Heard and Be Trusted*.

It's best that investors test the startup leader because they want to know answers to: "Can you succeed? Are you trustworthy?"

Recently, an interviewer asked me, "What's the biggest thing that an introvert could do to just screw up the whole thing?"

"Fail to rehearse," I replied.

In my *Convince Investors to Fund You* workshop, I truly like helping people rehearse during the workshop. I recall this quote:

I hear, and I forget.
I see, and I remember.
I do, and I understand.
– Confucius

What Do Investors Want to Know About You so They Find You to be Trustworthy?

In an interview, I said, "Investors want to know that you're trustworthy. And to know that you're stable." That got a chuckle from the interviewer.

Recently, I gave a workshop, *Convince Investors to Fund You* at a Silicon Valley, CA. Conference featuring keynote addresses by Stanford University notables.

This caught my eye because I have taught MBA students at Stanford University twice.

Also, I served as a Pitch Judge (for the conference), working with fellow Pitch Judge Henry Wong (leader of Garage Technology Ventures, co-founded by Guy Kawasaki).

During my workshop, I shared the following "5 C's."

The 5 C's to Assure Investors that You Are Trustworthy

1. Confident
2. Competent
3. Connection-building
4. Conflict-skilled
5. Coachable

1. Confident

To be perceived as confident, you do well to make sure that your words and body language are congruent.

Notice if your words do not match your hand gestures. If you say, "I'm confident that my new XY product will gain a 67% market share in two months" —but you're wringing your hands, there's a real problem. Your wringing hands *communicate your nervousness and self-doubt* more powerfully than your words might imply confidence.

The solution is to pay attention and act in positive ways. If you have a habit of wringing your hands, get your hands away from each other.

If you feel nervous, make sure that you have a 3 x 5 card in your hand and not an 8.5 x 11-inch sheet of paper in your hand. Why? A sheet of paper will betray the trembling of your hand.

If someone asks a tough question, pay attention and avoid your feet unconsciously betraying you by stepping back.

Instead, *practice taking two steps toward the person* and say something like "I can see that is important to you."

The above are just a few examples of how you can make your words and body language congruent—so they tell *one* story. The story is: You are confident. Confidence is contagious.

Here's something I often emphasize:
Confidence is not comfort.
Confidence is a toolkit, and you work it.

2. Competent

When one wants to signal to investors that he or she is competent—particularly in a pitch, it's best to use something I call the B.E.C.C. process.

In a pitch, you communicate with these elements:
B – big idea
E – engage with story
C – credible
C – compelling

Here we'll focus on the Big Idea. My short, memorable way to look at a Big Idea is "Unfair advantage, disruption and big profits." From my conversations with investors, I see that these three elements seize their attention.

The highly competent person delivering a pitch provides the Big Idea early in their pitch.

3. Connection-building

Demonstrate your finesse in building warm connections. Make the investor feel good as they talk with you. How? *Listen.*

Investors need to trust that you know how to build strong relationships. Great CEOs attract great talent and retain that talent. Great CEOs build coalitions throughout the company and with the board of directors.

Now, I'll share a tough time that helped me learn the lesson of the essential nature of connection-building.

A Real-Life Example—and Be Careful
about Connection-Building

In this example, I note that if you're not skilled with networking, you're going to have serious trouble. And, if you're not adept at follow-up, you're not going to win.

For example, some years ago, I was raising money for one of my first major projects.

Here's how I describe this when I give a speech about it: (lightly edited transcript)

"I get invited to attend a screening of a feature film that was made with independent funding, not from a studio. So, there was an opportunity for me to be very observant. I know these folks are the investors. I should talk with them. I should at least get my brochure into their hand.

Oh, that'll be great. Because I think: They'll see the brochure, and say, "Great idea! Here's my money!"

That's not how it works.

I found each investor at the celebration party. I gave every one of them my brochures. I felt really good. But then I noticed that they all said that they didn't have a handy business card

They said something like: "Oh, just call my office." They were standoffish.

That should teach me something.

They were there to celebrate that they had participated in getting this other film made. They were NOT there to have someone impose upon them. I was not creating good relationships.

Still, I was in my 20s when I was doing this—so it's

understandable that I lacked experience and understanding.

The next day I get a phone call from my production budget mentor. He was teaching me how to do the production budget for making my own feature film. But he taught me nothing about how to develop rapport or network with investors.

So, the production budget guy said on the phone, "I need to talk to you this afternoon. I'll meet you at my home."

I agreed.

He had me sit at his kitchen table. He reached into his pocket and pulled out one of my brochures. So, an investor had given it to him. He tossed that brochure on the table.

Then he disdainfully slammed brochure after brochure on that table.

I wanted to melt into to his flooring and <u>just die</u> so I didn't have to think about how embarrassed I felt.

He said, "You will write an apology letter to my business partner." My budget-writing mentor was a co-producer on that film. This embarrassing situation was awful."

This brochure massacre made a huge impression on me that lasts to this day. In fact, one of my first books was titled *Be Heard and Be Trusted.*

I made it my mission to learn how to create good business relationships — relationships built on trust.

What can an introvert do to cause trouble for himself or herself?

The big mistake is to be too eager and to overwhelm the investor. Don't be deluded that if you just tell them the idea, they'll be amazed and reach for their checkbook

This "coming on too strong" problem can an overreaction from an introvert who is just trying too hard. It's like a pendulum hitting the opposite side.

Here's what is necessary. Become a great listener. To get the listening started, you need to ask suitable questions. For example, you could ask, "So, how did you get into investing?"

The investor might reply with something like: "You know, originally I was an entrepreneur, and I started a company. I thought once I have a truly successful company, I'm going to start investing—being an angel investor in other people's stuff. You know, just to keep the cycle going."

You can reply with something like: "Oh. Sounds great. Would you tell me about your first company and what got you excited about it?"

It's all about building rapport. What you need is something called *emotional intelligence.* Daniel Goleman and others have done much work related to emotional intelligence. I saw a quote from a website that reads "We define emotional intelligence as: Recognize, understand and manage our own emotions ... Recognize, understand and influence the emotions of others." (Tomer Strolight, president of the firm that offers this definition).

This definition can be a springboard for our conversation here. Back in my 20s, when I had the snafu of my giving brochures to investors, I demonstrated that I had *not* developed appropriate emotional intelligence yet. I crossed the line as I tried to get investors interested in my feature film at the celebration for someone else's film.

This experience served as a springboard for my studies and getting mentors.

I also learned how to move beyond a traditional viewpoint about "selling." This part of my journey led to my writing the book, *Relax, You Don't Have to Sell*—in which I share the process of "enrolling."

You enroll somebody; you invite them into what you're doing.

I shared the mess I made as a twenty-something person with my first project. I had come on too strong and self-focused with my brochures. That was in line with my then-picture of traditional selling.

Years later, in my book, *Relax, You Don't Have to Sell*, I note:

Selling is imposition.
Enrolling is invitation.

You invite the person into your world. That's the invitation part. Still, you do some great listening first. Then, the person might be interested in listening to you.

4. Conflict-skilled

"Tell me about a conflict you and your co-founders had and what happened," I said to a young guy looking for investors. He had stepped up to me after I had served as a Pitch Judge at a conference.

He replied, "No. We get along really well. It's great. Like we're brothers from another mother."

One of my friends in Silicon Valley, California noted a top startup company breaker: *co-founder conflict.*

Until you've had an argument with your co-founder, I don't know if your team will survive. Investors need to know that you're strong and skillful in leading to a resolution when conflict arrives.

Perhaps, you've noticed how several people like to control things by trying to use email or texts to state their position, and then they refuse to have a seven-minute in-person (or telephone) conversation.

The key to handling problems and conflict within an organization is to keep the channels of communication wide open.
– Anita Roddick

The truth is: Mature adults and good leaders talk to people they cannot stand.

By this I mean, the trustworthy leader, as Anita Roddick said, keeps the channel of communication wide open.

The Conflict-Skilled Person Knows When to Say, "I'll walk toward you."

The effective leader practices two important skills (among many others):

- Know when to stand your ground
- Know when to say, "I'll walk towards you."

Sometimes, you must hold your ground. An investor might ask, "Have you fired anyone? Have you ever fired a friend?"

If you can say yes to this, the investor often looks on you as a more seasoned professional.

Conflict-skilled Includes Being Able to Say No and to Find the Third Alternative

Recently, I heard a couple of people talking about *strength of character*. The idea was that a person needs to be able to say no. If that person cannot say *no*, he or she can be pushed around and even "argued into submission."

Even worse, I've seen people push others *to feel guilty.* How? One person says to an abusive father, "Hey, you're insulting me." And then a family member says, "You know that is Dad's way. Why are you causing conflict?"

Wait a minute. Who was abusive?—the father. But the person standing her ground is being dressed down for speaking her truth? This is trouble.

Earlier in this book, I shared information about crazy-makers. **Crazy-makers have no empathy.** You cannot change their mind by appealing to fairness or logic. So, in the situation when a family member defends a crazy-maker-father, there is no "nice" solution. Sometimes, you must simply state what is going on ("you're insulting me") and step back—to protect yourself.

In terms of business, if you find yourself with a crazy-maker co-founder, it may be necessary to part ways.

5. Coachable

Why do you to need prove that you're coachable to investors? Because investors have seen non-coachable people crash and burn and take their companies down with them.

Several investors sometimes see themselves in young people on their way up. Such investors have thoughts like: "Oh, you look like someone who is a 'young me' when I first started. I can save you from so many big mistakes."

It works best if you come across as all three: confident, competent *and coachable.* Some people are "tech-competent" and "people-clumsy."

Instead, a mature business person has all 5 Crucial Characteristics: Confident, Competent, Connection-building, Conflict-skilled and Coachable. That's a mature person.

Beware of How Certain CEOs Flame Out

Unfortunately, some CEOs flame out because they're not coachable, and they're not connection-building. They make "bold decisions" that fail because they had no devoted effort building coalitions and support.

Ultimately, the Board of Directors fires them because they're not successful at building connections with the board directors. I refer to this process as a form of "CEO suicide."

What the Start-up CEO Needs to Be Ready For

Often, after I serve as a Pitch Judge, start-up company leaders come up and ask questions.

Some of them just jump in with, "So who do you know who would like to invest in what I pitched?" Sometimes, my thoughts jump to "oh, another amateur." By this I mean, this person did the "amateur" thing of failing to build rapport first. Then they want me to stick my neck out and risk sharing one of my great contacts with someone who is not adept at building rapport and connections.

Still, I strive to be helpful. So, I ask a few questions:

- How much money do you need?
- What have you finished?
- Have you and your co-founders experienced a big disagreement yet?

Many newbies to fundraising choke on the "how much do you need?" question. The solution is to think it through and know multiple levels of money and what you can accomplish.

It sounds like:

- For $200,000 we can get this done ...
- For $500,000, we can get this done and ____ and ____ ...

About the Question "What have you finished?"

This is a telling question. The savvy start-up leader does

well to have a list of three things that he or she has finished. Why? Because we want a company leader who can stick with a project, lead people, complete the project and get results.

Have References

I'll make this detail brief: Have at least three people who say, "Yes. I would definitely work [him/her] again, given the opportunity."

Demonstrate You're Coachable by Covering Your "Gaps"

We realize that no human being can do the whole thing by himself or herself. The smart leaders look at how they can "cover their gaps." In my book, *Shape the Future, Lead Like a Pro*, I refer to smart leaders as *RoiLeaders* (who specialize in "Relate, Optimize, Intuit).

The RoiLeader demonstrates that they are truly competent by admitting their gaps and hiring people to shore up these areas.

The smartest thing I ever did was to hire my weakness.
– Sara Blakely

Incompetent people either try to cover up weakness or they might be delusional and think they do not have any weakness.

The good news is that the RoiLeader is coachable.

The Coachable Person is Trustworthy

When networking, you get people to like you by *listening first.*

The classic idea is that one wants a new person to know

you, like you and trust you.

For example, Ross Perot invested in Steve Jobs' company, NeXT. Perot said that he really was investing in Steve Jobs.

Investors are looking for someone they can trust to lead a company they invest in. Why? Many companies must pivot fast before launch and when the first version of a product gets into the marketplace. The leader must often scramble to energize members to make last-minute changes.

For example, a company had a good plan. They would launch eight products and see what worked. They wisely realized that some products would fail. They were fortunate: Project #2 was the Thighmaster that generated more than $100 million in sales. This was their second project, but they were ready to go through eight projects.

Here's a story that illustrates the pattern of what often happens in the marketplace:

Sandy decides, "I'm going to sell ice cream and people are going to eat with these spoons. Then, Sandy gets surprised. Customers say, "The ice cream is okay, but those spoons! We love those spoons. They're fantastic." Sandy has her company do a pivot.

What's great about small start-up companies is that a good CEO can make a fast decision and jump on an opportunity.

In summary ...

Recently, I asked my co-host on my podcast *Introverts Own Your Voice* (on iTunes and YouTube), "What will you take forward from our conversation about the 5 C's?"

She replied: "I think the biggest thing is that the investor doesn't just invest in your project or idea, they're investing in you and your capabilities."

List of the *Five Exercises*

At my workshop, *Convince Investors to Fund You*, I use five exercises. The attendees rehearse powerful actions, and this process transforms their approach to critical situations. Here I will share brief descriptions of the exercises. (Participating in the exercises in-person at the workshop provides the best experience.)

1. **Confident** – Exercise 1
   Congruent-Walk Toward the Question. The purpose of this exercise is to give the workshop attendees the experience of holding their body language in a confident manner even though they're in an uncomfortable situation. They practice saying, "I can see how that is important to you" while they walk *toward* the person who asked the question.

2. **Competent** – Exercise 2
   Express the Big Idea. The purpose of this exercise is to practice clearly expressing a Big Idea that captures the attention of investors. Attendees practice expressing their Big Idea with these 3 Elements: Unfair advantage, disruption and big profits.

3. **Connection-building** – Exercise 3
   Positive Small Talk. The purpose of this exercise is to practice asking a question that does *not* feel invasive to the investor—upon first meeting. An invasive question can sound like "What are you looking for in an investment?" That is putting the investor "on the spot." Instead, we ask, when appropriate, a *gentle question* in a friendly tone: "So, how did you get into investing?"

4. **Conflict-skilled** – Exercise 4

   Positive Story about Conflict. The purpose of this exercise is to have the workshop attendee practice describing how he or she led a team to a positive resolution of a conflict-laden situation. The pattern is to tell a Positive Story with these elements: "My point is that I'm good at leading people through a conflict situation. For example, the conflict was _____, and I led the positive resolution by doing ____. And the great results were _____." The extraordinary leader ably guides team members through conflict because conflict can often lead to better solutions, better products and better engagement with clients.

5. **Coachable** – Exercise 5

   "Mentor Guided Me" Story. The purpose of this exercise is to help the workshop attendee form and express a story that demonstrates that the person responds well to coaching, takes direction and achieves excellent results. This dispels the investor's concern that the startup leader may be too ego-centered to face reality and learn from others. The pattern is to say something like: "One of my mentors guided me with _____. And when I implemented what they suggested, the great result was ____. My point is: I make certain that I am coachable."

   * * * * * *

Special Notes about Follow-up:

- Be brief.
- Respond quickly and be consistent.
- Target to fulfill what the person has already

communicated as important to them.

- Identify what their workstyle preferences are. By this I mean, find out if they prefer email, text, Skype or in-person meetings and other such details.

To make this memorable, I developed the W.I.N. process:

W – work their workstyle preferences
I – integrate investor's priorities
N – nurture investor's impressions

1. Work their workstyle preferences

It's vital for you to identify as soon as possible the investors workstyle preferences. You avoid crossing a line and losing the investor. For example, you might encounter an investor who is trying to save his or her marriage and has decided that the hours between 6 pm and 8 pm are only for family.

If you call between the hours of 6 and 8, you may be on the receiving end of the investor's intense anger—even if you hadn't received this information earlier.

Additionally, related to workstyle preferences: Some people prefer email and texting. Others prefer in-person meetings. Some people reserve weekends for their families.

You can get information about an investor's workstyle preferences by asking something like: "When I work with someone, I always like to find out what their workstyle preferences are. And in this way things go smoothly. I don't make an error and call you at the wrong time. Or if you prefer email, I focus on providing what information you need in the way you prefer to receive it."

2. Integrate investor's priorities

It's vital for you to make your communications focused on the investor's priorities. Anything else will be noise or pollution to the investor. On the subconscious mind level, the investor is likely to consider you an amateur. Once that impression takes root, you have a huge problem. The way to get around this is to be sure to ask questions that often take the form of *"What's most important to you about...?"*

3. Nurture investor's impressions

The more you know about the investor's impressions of you, your offering and other pertinent details, you are better able to nurture the relationship.

You can ask questions like:

- What do you like the most about this investment opportunity?
- What do you like the most about investing with me?
- I like to learn. If you had a moment to coach me, what would you bring to my attention? [You create the impression that you are coachable. A classic idea is: "Ask for funding and you get advice. Ask for advice and you get funding."]

Power Principle:

Investors will trust you and fund your project when they know you demonstrate the 5 C's: Confident, Competent, Connection-building, Conflict-skilled, and Coachable.

Power Questions:

Have you identified how you may be lacking in the 5 C's? What specifically can you do to enhance how you are perceived as Confident, Competent, Connection-building, Conflict-skilled, and Coachable?

The Savvy CEO Wins

Whoever renders service to many puts himself in line for greatness—great wealth, great return, great satisfaction, great reputation, and great joy. – Jim Rohn

Here are some brief details about the insights and distinctions that I share with my clients and audience members who are CEOs.

These materials help the Savvy CEO win. CEOs whom I've interviewed and the CEOs whom I have coached are people who like to win. They like to win more often, and they like to win more efficiently.

For any CEO or other business leader who has a concern that they won't perform at their best in front of the media, in an all-hands meeting. addressing the board of directors, attracting extraordinary talent and retaining extraordinary talent, this section has valuable guidance.

We'll use the C.E.O.S. process:

C – choose the premise
E – empower answers to 10 Worst Questions
O – overprepare with Recovery Methods
S – start with listening

1. Choose the Premise

Even the most complicated stories start with a very simple premise. – Chris Van Allsburg

If you're interacting with the media, you'll notice that some individuals (part of the media) seek to pin a particular premise on you which can hurt you. Their goals are to increase their ratings and increase the drama. Do *not* accept their premise.

A classic example of a terrible premise is when someone in the media asks, "Do you still beat your spouse?" Your answer is: "I always treat my spouse with kindness and respect. So, it looks like George has a question."

The idea is that you avoid repeating any words that can be recorded as a sound bite that will be used against you. You choose the premise. You state only details that will benefit your cause.

2. Empower answers to the 10 Worst Questions

By failing to prepare, you are preparing to fail.
– Benjamin Franklin

Preparing yourself for *the 10 Worst Questions the media are likely to ask,* gives you an advantage. I guide my clients to prepare at least two answers for each Worst Question. That means that the client has 20 prepared answers. Excellent. The client is more prepared than many people facing a press event.

A certain number of situations a CEO faces have predictable elements. If you're going to face the media, you will likely be confronted with some horrible questions designed to create truly *clickable links* on the Internet.

I have my clients uncover their best words so that they are ready for terrible questions. The idea is to provide yourself with two answers for each terrible question so then you come in *over prepared* and ready to answer the 10 Worst Questions.

3. Over prepare with Recovery Methods

Spectacular achievement is always preceded by unspectacular preparation. – Robert H. Schuller

Over the years in teaching MBA students (including at Stanford University), I teach public speaking by beginning with Recovery Methods. Why? If you know how to recover, your level of nervousness goes significantly down.

Here's an example of a *Recovery Method*. You say, "I need to pause for a moment. I want my response to be valuable to you." Using this phrase helps you get critical time to think through your answer before you say anything. The Savvy CEO wins by being well-spoken. How? You pause and avoid blurting out something that could hurt you.

Here's another Recovery Method. During a speech I gave at IBM, I got stuck. I wasn't certain what the next two sentences would be. So, I said, "I need to pause for a moment, my brain needs more RAM." They thought that was hilarious—a Random Access Memory bit of humor.

The point is: When you're ready to respond to some difficulty in a speech, you use a Recovery Method. You come across as poised and confident. That is the posture of The Savvy CEO.

4. Start with listening

We have two ears and one mouth so that we can listen twice as much as we speak. – Epictetus

The Savvy CEO knows that leaders who do the best have the best intel. You need to know about the best ideas. You must know what's going on, what's going wrong, and how to fix situations. The Savvy CEO makes sure to ask appropriate questions and then this CEO does a lot of listening.

I work with creative teams. So, I refrain from offering my opinions first. Why? Because I want to get ideas and perceptions that differ from my own. This further empowers my decision-making process.

I'll ask questions like:

- How are things going?
- What are your thoughts and feelings about this?
- What's working?
- What can be improved?
- Where is a potential bottleneck to the process?
- What do you need from me, so you can do your best work?

Now it's your turn. What can you ask to set people at ease and then learn what is really going on?

Power Principle:

The Savvy CEO over prepares and has his or her Recovery Methods well-rehearsed.

Power Questions:

Are you developing the skills to ask appropriate questions and do a lot of listening? As you do more listening are you seeing team members connect with you more? Are you prepared with "not accepting the premise" when interacting with the media?

Bonus Material:

Focus Points for Big Progress

Many people are programmed to dislike those people who seek financial abundance. *Measure by your heart, not by their approval.*

Perhaps, you noticed that some people scoff at you when you guard your personal budget by choosing to eat burritos at a small restaurant instead having a fancy, expensive dinner elsewhere.

You need to stay true to your own personal goals.

One affirmation I heard goes: "Money comes to me easily, and my wealth continues to grow." To do well moneywise, you'll need to be adept with savings. Focus on acquiring skills, taking bold action and staying in *Accumulation Mode*.

Many people shy away from conflict. Your answer to create wealth is: Become conflict-skilled. If you're dealing with a naysaying family member, you could say things like:

- I hear you.
- Okay. (You are *not* agreeing. You are just noting that you heard the statement someone said.)
- Maybe so.

For those of us who are in our own Accumulation Mode, protect your time and avoid trying to "convert" someone to your point of view about service and financial abundance.

Many people were brainwashed to be against earning great sums of money. So be it. Avoid letting their limits hinder you in any way.

Choose your own way. Implement methods from this book.

Focus Points for Big Progress #1

Choose to do *Great Service* and Accumulate Wealth

What if you could unshackle yourself from the limiting beliefs that sabotage you from taking the best actions?

How about dropping the limiting thoughts that hold you back from accumulating great wealth? **If you shift your thoughts to creating great service, you will have an advantage. You will release the brake.**

Whoever renders service to many puts himself in line for greatness—great wealth, great return, great satisfaction, great reputation, and great joy. – Jim Rohn

Getting rich is less about intellect and more about focusing on the accumulation of wealth. – Steve Siebold

Recently, I stepped down from the stage, having served on a panel of Pitch Judges. One person approached me with an idea that would help volunteers better serve those in need. And, I had the thought that, maybe, this might be a great humanitarian endeavor.

Many things are worth doing even if one cannot get paid.

However, this is a book about becoming rich and smart. So, consider finding ways to serve many people *and* open the gate to good profits.

To get rich, you have to be making money while you're asleep.
– David Bailey

Everything you want in life is reachable only if you start [sales] prospecting like your life depends on it. ... I had to knock on thousands of cold doors just to get people to even know me when I started my first business. That is the main purpose of prospecting—to get people to know about you. – Grant Cardone

Power Principle:
Doing great service that benefits the lives of many opens the door to accumulating wealth.

Power Questions:
Do you really want financial abundance? Are you making the tough choices to focus on what brings great service to many people—and what creates a great cash flow? Are you prospecting, that is, getting people to know you?

Focus Points for Big Progress #2

Focus and Use Time Well

The only difference between a rich person and a poor person is how they use their time. – Robert Kiyosaki

Imagine you felt proud of yourself. And, you saw tangible progress. More money in your bank account. More time free of money worries. Are you in?

Time management is *not* what we're looking for. Instead, we're looking for results. More than that, we're looking to experience positive feelings. And, many of us feel that if we somehow got our time management right, we'd achieve so much.

I've learned with working with clients and MBA students that there's something better than making a list and using standard time management techniques. It's called *effective Self-leadership.* We want to overcome procrastination and the misguided, clumsy use of our personal time.

Time is more valuable than money. You can get more money, but you cannot get more time. – Jim Rohn

I've written three books tackling time management issues:
- *Time Management Secrets the Rich Won't Tell You*
- *Power Time Management: More Time, Less Stress, and Zero Procrastination (Your Breakthrough for More Success, Happiness and Time Off)*
- *Soar! Nothing Can Stop You This Year*

I've learned that setting empowering systems beats falling back on a vague notion of trying to use willpower.

I've dropped 15 lbs. in 48 days and kept them off. I found **using systems** made it possible.

Keep score and achieve more. – Tom Marcoux

Here is one of my systems. Before I go to sleep each night, I write, on a 3 x 5 card, a list called *Top Six Targets.* When I address an audience I often say, "2 for you, 2 for family, 2 for work." This is a method to make sure that you do the most important things during the next day.

Power Principle:
We don't want time management—instead we want valuable results. We need strategy and Self-leadership.

Power Questions:
What holds you back? How do your habits cause you to procrastinate? Have you identified systems so that you do not have to attempt to use willpower to get things done? What new action will you take so that you more effectively get things done?

Focus Points for Big Progress #3

Move Forward with Courage

Before you can become a millionaire, you must learn to think like one. You must learn how to motivate yourself to counter fear with courage. – Thomas J. Stanley

In working with several coaches and mentors I have repeatedly heard the question: "What are you most proud of yourself for?"

Additionally, we get at the deeper meaning with this question: "What do you most want to be in a eulogy about you?"

I realized that I am proud of myself for my courage.

Courage is often defined as being afraid and doing it, anyway. I've noticed that my clients often feel exhilarated when they take action with courage. They are so proud of themselves. This is only experienced when we stretch ourselves, and we get into the arena. Sometimes I say, "You must get into the arena."

Fortune favors the bold. – Virgil

I'd get kicked out of buildings all day long, people would rip up my business card in my face. It's a humbling business to be in. But I knew I could sell, and I knew I wanted to sell something I had created. I cut the feet out of those pantyhose, and I knew I was on to something. This was it. – Sara Blakely

Often, to become rich, you must step into uncharted territory.

I'd never worked in fashion or retail. I just needed an undergarment that didn't exist." – Sara Blakely

Instead of failure being the outcome, failure became not trying. And it forced me at a young age to want to push myself so much further out of my comfort zone. – Sara Blakely

The people who have never lost are afraid of losing. They're afraid of learning. They're afraid of that terrible feeling you get from losing. ... Bombing on stage took me to another place because I realized that I never want to feel that feeling again. So, I ramped everything up. I went back to my notebooks and I went back to work. ... I figured out what I was doing wrong and I tried to improve upon it. – Joe Rogan

Joe Rogan is a comedian whose humor works for some and does not work for others. Still, he tells us the truth about the hard facts of gaining success as a comedian.

Successful people learn to face the possibility of losing. Then press onward and get "into the arena" where you can gain a client or lose a client.

In fact, I developed a principle for myself and clients:

If you have one and you lose one, it's a tragedy.

If you have twenty and you lose one, it's just a step.

I also guide my audiences and clients with these ideas:

Confidence is not comfort.

Confidence is a toolkit, and you work it.

At one point, I was doing a Solo-Reflection session getting ready for a session with a client. My intuition gave me this question: **"Are you in crisis or in recommitment?"**

My point in sharing this question with my client was to help the person see the opportunity. Working with clients over months, I see them hit a point where they feel pressed. They may feel tired and discouraged. But if they take the chance to make a recommitment, *they rise to the level of more achievement and feeling proud of themselves.*

They learn that real happiness and life satisfaction arises when one moves forward with courage.

Power Principle:

Move forward with courage.

Power Questions:

What do you want so much that you're willing to dig deep for courage? What is the source of your energy to get things done?

Focus Points for Big Progress #4

Being Prepared for the Worst Often Gets You the Best

Wealth is largely the result of habit. – John Jacob Astor

The center of much of my work is *Words – Strategy – Rehearsal.* Rehearsal is crucial because I am focused on helping my clients experience a *transformation.* We're *not* looking for a Band-Aid provided by an idea. We are looking for increasing the capabilities of the individual.

Rehearsal is required for extraordinary accomplishments. Before Navy Seals accomplish any mission, they run many cycles of training and practice. My focus is on making sure that my client experiences being *over prepared.* We run many rehearsals in which they must use Recovery Methods to stay poised when under extreme stress of giving the most high-level presentation.

For many [people], the acquisition of wealth does not end their troubles, it only changes them. – Lucius Annaeus Seneca

Many people may look upon having to do a lot of rehearsal as a "new problem." However, when you want financial freedom, you will do what is necessary. You'll train "like a Navy Seal" in your own methods (in your own industry).

Spectacular achievement is always preceded by unspectacular preparation. – Robert H. Schuller

Power Principle:
Being prepared for the worst often gets you the best.

Power Questions:
What is the worst thing that could happen? How can you do some preparations, so you have the best chance to make something turn out better than your first impression?

Focus Points for Big Progress #5

Prepare Yourself for the Surprise Opportunity—and Be Alert

I got a call from the Oprah Winfrey Show. Oprah had chosen Spanx as one of her favorite products in 2000. I had boxes of product in my apartment, and I had two-weeks' notice that she was going to say she loved it on TV, and I had no shipping department. – Sara Blakely

Energy and imagination are the springboards to wealth creation. – Brian Tracy

**To Be Ready for the Surprise Opportunity,
You Must Be Present and Alert**

Recently, I came across this quote:

Successful people control their inner dialogue. – Brian Tracy

I had several thoughts and feelings about this. Is it possible to control the rush of thoughts in one's head? We note that thoughts lead to feelings. Feeling can shut us down and paralyze us—or lift us up to great achievement and wealth.

Then I came across these details: Marianne Williamson tells the story of her friend Naomi Warren who endured two years of her life in Auschwitz. Upon her liberation (at twenty-three), she concentrated on this thought, "Hitler got two years of my life. He will *not* get another day."

Naomi's experience plus her focus point and Brian Tracy's quotes inspired me to entertain new thoughts.

Naomi made a choice in terms of how she was going to direct her thoughts. We can imagine that anytime she thought, *Hitler—I hate that man!* she could override it by saying, "You will *not* get it another day."

So, the idea here is that you may not be able to control what thoughts come up, but **you can condition yourself with some type of trigger.**

You'll use that *Self-created Trigger* to shift the direction of your thoughts. *This is where you find your freedom of choice.*

Pick what you want to use as a statement or question so that you can shift the direction of your thoughts and then make sure that you stay present and alert.

Here are examples:

- Does this strengthen me? How can I take better care of myself?
- What would be the healthy choice here?

People who are obsessed with the past or caught up in

bitterness fail to see the opportunities that are in the surrounding landscape.

In summary …

An important part of you preparing yourself for the surprise opportunity is to study and to *condition yourself to be at your best in the present moment.* I have a number of *self-created triggers* so that I can shift to a state of being in which I can be most productive.

Now it's your turn. Do you want to develop your own *self-created triggers* to take control of your day?

Power Principle:
Be present and alert so you jump at a surprise opportunity.

Power Questions:
How are you removing distractions from your life? How are you guarding your personal energy? In what areas are you devoting time to study and practice, so you can jump at surprise opportunities?

Focus Points for Big Progress #6

"What reality do you need to face and how are you bringing your A Game to it?"

Truth will always be truth, regardless of lack of understanding, disbelief or ignorance. – W. Clement Stone

Have the courage to say no. Have the courage to face the truth. Do the right thing because it is right. These are the magic keys to living your life with integrity. – W. Clement Stone

Life is hard. The classic idea is: If someone tells you, life is not hard, they're either delusional or trying to sell you something.

So, what do we do with that? Perhaps, you notice the dysfunctional approaches of hiding, denying and getting bitter. Add getting paralyzed and being victimized, and you get the grim picture.

This is NOT for you.

Take an Empowered Stance for Life. Face reality and devote yourself to putting full-energy into training, study and conditioning yourself to increase your wisdom and personal strength.

Sometimes, "Trying Hard" is not as important as *empower yourself and open your eyes.*

Doing the same thing, but more of it, can be the wrong plan. Some people fail with Facebook ads, but then *change their approach* and find a personal touch with connecting one-to-one with people on LinkedIn works better.

Some years ago, I was on the phone with a clerk on the line. I told the truth: "I really appreciate your help with this. You see, I don't get paid by the hour. I get paid by results. So, your help with this gives me the chance to get back to what my client really wants me to focus on."

One of my mentors said, "The ideal plan is to devote 50% of your efforts to cash flow and 50% of your efforts to building assets ... during your week."

One of the key secrets if you really want to become wealthy: get in front of a trend. – Tony Robbins

How do you get in front of a trend? You need to stay strong and keep alert.

Here are examples of *Reality You Need to Face:*
- Not placing phone calls to enough prospective clients
- Not improving your skills for closing a sale
- Not scheduling time for your personal, healthy habits

Here are examples of *Bringing Your A Game:*
- Set goals on three levels Good-Excellent-Amazing! (example: marketing calls .... Good (5), Excellent (10), Amazing! (21) ... for the week
- Get an Executive Coach and refine your sales presentations and next speeches
- Rehearse your speech every day (at least 9 minutes in the morning and 9 minutes at night)*

* For example, before I presented my workshop *Convince Investor to Fund You*, I rehearsed in front of a team member 27 times. (During those sessions which could have been as short as 20 minutes, I found the humor bits and concise language to make my points.)

Power Principle:
Consider this: "What reality do you need to face and how you are bringing your A Game to it?"

Power Questions:
What is a tough reality that you're facing? What can you do to improve your approach? Do you need to get coaching

to raise the level of your game in this area?

Special Bonus Material:

Here are some highlights of principles, secrets and methods for having dinner with notable people. Use these methods to build rapport and open the door to having new clients.

The first principle is: *When you're listening, you're winning.* How do we get them to talk and feel comfortable with us? You avoid going straight into a business-conversation.

You can use the following questions:

- So, how are things going for you?
- Oh, I'm curious. Is there something you're looking forward to?
- So, I'm wondering. What is one of your hobbies—you know, something that you do to relax?

When you ask somebody *is there something you're looking forward to?* the person often asks, "In business or a vacation?"

"Oh—whichever you prefer talk about," I reply. The idea is that you want them to have a good time talking with you. They can feel something tied to: "Wow. I have a new audience. Someone who hasn't heard all my old stories. This is fun."

What to do if you're not seated next to someone who would be an ideal person to speak with

If you're not seated next to the most important person your intuition is telling you that it's best for you approach, use these following methods.

- Walk up in a comfortable style to the notable person and their conversation companion. And say, "Something tells me that it would be good for me to talk with you two."
- Listen to the other person continue to express their ideas to the notable person.
- Pick something to praise in what the other person says and share your appreciation. (You'll make a friend as the other person enjoys the praise. Secondly, the notable person appreciates how respectful and polite you are to that other person.)
- At an appropriate time, turn to the notable person and ask some questions like: "So, I'm curious. How is this conference going for you? Was there some part of it that you were looking forward to?—and did you get what you were hoping to get?"

Here are some special additional methods:

If possible, do something kind for the notable person. If they're sitting across from you, you can pass them something, perhaps, a shared dish. Your plan is to be gracious. For example, as a feature film producer-director in Hollywood, I had a sushi dinner with an actor, a regular cast member of the TV show *E.R.* This actor poured soy sauce into the little dish, which is part of the process of eating sushi. The reason why I share this information is because I never forgot that gracious, little gesture.

Here's another method. If possible, ask the notable person to pass you something—perhaps, the salt or a sauce. This method helps the notable person to feel, on the subconscious level, something tied to: "Oh, we're friendly. We're just breaking bread together."

Special note: We want the notable person to feel like you're just being friends—and you are peers. Be careful that you don't come across as a step below them or as subservient—or as a supplicant. You need to go with your intuition about what's good for creating rapport.

How to slip in some details that promote your business without derailing the conversation and breaking rapport

The first principle is that you make your comment brief, like 15 seconds. Then you immediately ask a gentle question to return the spotlight of the conversation onto the other person.

Here's an example:

The person asks, "So, what do you do?"

You reply: "Since you mentioned that you've had a great improvement in your business over the last two months … I do something that, actually, you might find interesting. I help top business owners reduce stress, increase income, and take guilt-free vacations. I'm wondering … What is something about your business that really makes you smile."

Some Insights about Experiencing Happiness

Rich and happy—sound good, right?

Beware that having *certain rules* in your mind will *block* your having the space to experience happy moments.

We do not remember days, we remember moments.

– Cesare Pavese

Recently, I glanced at one of my previous books and saw my reference to an old phrase: *"Happiness is something to do, someone to love and something to hope for."*

Just today, I coached a client, Andrew, and said, "Someone comes to you for two things: *hope and certainty.* They ask, *Can you help me?* **Yes.** No hesitation. And your certainty is that you're all in. You're going to do your best to help them rise to a higher level in life."

What prevents rising to a higher level in life? Holding onto "rules" that kill your happiness. Some of the rules seem logical. For example, can you be happy and physically ill? I've seen that this is possible. Sometimes, I have said, "My spirit is good; my body is catching up."

I am *not* holding a rule that I must be pain-free to be happy.

Here are examples of **Happiness-Killing Rules:**
- I can't be happy if I have any pain.
- Happiness must be a whole day.
- If someone yells at me, that ruins my whole day.
- I must achieve to be happy.

- I must relax, or I must be on a vacation to be happy.
- Work only hurts—there is no joy in work.
- Things are scarce in this world.
- There is only win, lose, and compromise.*

* Author Stephen R. Covey suggested that we can, in a continued dialogue, find a "3rd Alternative"—a solution that can help both people receive benefits that they personally desire.

In recent conversations with several friends on the topic of happiness, I've gathered that there are at least five aspects or **Facets to Happiness: Joy contentment, fulfillment, satisfaction, and relief (comfort).**

Several people imply that being rich and being happy do not line up.

You can only become truly accomplished at something you love. Don't make money your goal. Instead, pursue the things you love doing, and then do them so well that people can't take their eyes off you. – Maya Angelou

Maya Angelou's above quote relates to the facets of *fulfillment and satisfaction.*

The idea that "rich and being happy do not line up" is just a flimsy idea. **Instead, you can arrange your life in the way you choose.**

Let's continue.

Joy relates to joyful moments—the moments of fun and enthusiasm.

Contentment relates to a quiet enjoyment—a quiet experience of good feelings.

Fulfillment often arises out of sense of meaning and that you're making some movement towards doing things that are meaningful in your life.

Satisfaction can arise for someone who seeks to be prosperous from coming up with ways to serve, delivering that service and then reaping the benefits of financial abundance as people purchase and enjoy what one offers.

Relief was a facet mentioned by one of my friends. He has no interest in the whole process of becoming prosperous. This friend is only interested in comfort and only talks about doing tasks in the terms of relieving stress or tension.

Years ago, some authors spoke of the difference between tension-relieving and goal-achieving. Goal-achieving is related to Satisfaction. Are you satisfied with your life? Are you satisfied with what you're accomplishing?

I include this section to acknowledge that being rich does not guarantee feeling happy.

The only thing money gives you is the freedom of not worrying about money. – Johnny Carson

I'll add that such freedom from worry frees up your personal energy. *That is truly valuable.*

In such a state of freedom, you have more likelihood of being able to enjoy the *5 Facets of Happiness: Joy, contentment, fulfillment, satisfaction and relief (comfort).*

In a number of my books I have written: "Confidence is not comfort. Confidence is a tool kit and you work it." Let's look at having a personal tool kit related to happiness.

Money is multiplied in practical value depending on the number of W's you control in your life: what you do, when you do it, where you do it, and with whom you do it. – Tim Ferriss

In many ways, the journey of rich *and* happy is about nurturing your personal energy.

If you are dead inside, the other person can do a lot of things for Valentine, it won't make a dent. There is nobody at the reception desk. [So, the questions are] "I turn myself on when... I wake up when..." – Esther Perel

Ester Perel addresses long-term romantic relationships. Still, the insight that we must turn on and nurture our own personal energy applies to much of life.

So, let's pull together some related ideas.

Look to what gives you the experiences of happy moments. See how you can look at the 5 facets of Happiness and avoid setting "rules" that prevent you from having some moments of happiness each day. Focus on how you can have a daily experience, in some form, of Joy, Contentment, Fulfillment, Satisfaction and Relief (comfort).

Finally, several philosophies and spiritual paths note, "At the end of your life, you will ask, did I live fully and love well?"

For a full experience of happiness, be sure to live fully and love well. *The best to you.*

Introverts Own Your Voice™

with Tom Marcoux
Episodes on YouTube
Podcast on iTunes

The **Introvert's Formula to Get Clients**™

3-Week Session

- **Experience Real Confidence**
- **Learn to Gain Trust Quickly**
- **Gain Clients Effectively**
- **Rehearse with a Partner – So the Techniques *Become Part of You***
- **Overcome Procrastination**
- **Let Go of Fear and Nervousness**
- **Handle Tough Moments (even if your mind goes blank)**

Online Course

Seen & Heard:
abc
Stanford University
KCBS 740 AM—FM 106.9

Tom Marcoux
Spoken Word Strategist

Contact:
TomSuperCoach@gmail.com

137

A Final Word and the Springboard

Congratulations on your efforts with this book.

Please consider continuing to work with me through my **executive coaching** (phone and in-person), workshops and keynote addresses. Visit my blogs:

PitchPowerFest.com

GetTheBigYES.com

TheSavvyCEOWins.com

YourBodySoulandProsperity.com

Enjoy my YouTube Channel *Introverts Own Your Voice* (podcast on iTunes).

Meanwhile, *to get even more value from this book,* take the plans and insights that you created and place them in some form in your calendar or day planner. *Plan and take action.* Return to these pages again and again to reconnect with the material and take your life to higher levels.

The best to you,

Tom

Tom Marcoux

Spoken Word Strategist

CEO, Executive Coach—Pitch Coach

Special Offer Just for Readers of this Book:

Contact Tom Marcoux at tomsupercoach@gmail.com for special discounts on coaching, books, workshops and presentations. Just mention your experience with this book.

Apply for a FREE Breakthrough Strategy Session—see the VIDEO at TomSuperCoach.com/breakthrough

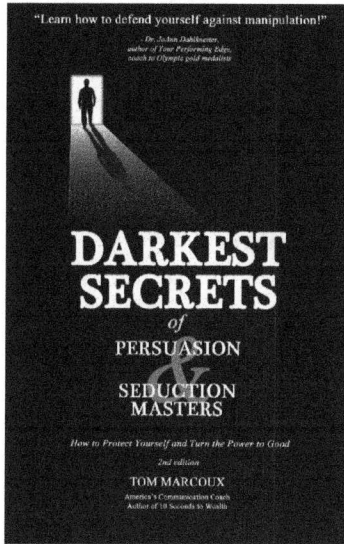

Excerpt from

Darkest Secrets of Persuasion and Seduction Masters: How to Protect Yourself and Turn the Power to Good

by Tom Marcoux, Executive Coach – Spoken Word Strategist
Copyright Tom Marcoux

. . . Now, I am in my 40's, with gray in my hair, and for 27 years I have been taking action to protect people.

And now is the time for me to protect you with the Countermeasures I reveal in this book.

Every human being needs to be able to break the trance that a Manipulator creates. You need to make good decisions so you are safe and you keep growing—and you are not cut down and crippled.

This Darkest Secrets material is so intense that I first released it only with the counterbalance of my most energizing and uplifting books, *Soar! Nothing Can Stop You This Year* and *Year of Awesome: How You Can Use 12 Success*

Principles including 10 Seconds to Wealth.

An interviewer asked me: "Who can be the Manipulator?"

A co-worker, a boss, a salesperson, someone you're dating, and someone you think is a friend.

Now is the time—this very minute—for me to write this book to protect you.

I must speak the truth.

These Darkest Secrets of "persuasion masters" are …

Wait a minute! Let's say it plainly: These are the Darkest Secrets of masters of manipulation. Throughout this book, I will call these people what they are: Manipulators.

Dictionary.com defines "manipulate" as "To influence or manage shrewdly or deviously…. To tamper with or falsify for personal gain."

In this book, we will look on a manipulator as one who deviously influences someone with no concern about that person's well-being, and who causes harm to that person.

Here is the first Darkest Secret:

Darkest Secret #1:

Manipulators Make You Hurt
and Then Offer the Salve.

Manipulators would invite you to go out in the sun for hours and then sell you the salve to soothe your burns. The problem is that we don't notice that this is what they're doing.

For example, you're considering the purchase of a house. A Manipulator asks the question, "So, where would you put your TV?" This question is designed to put you into a trance.

Dictionary.com defines "trance" as "a half-conscious state, seemingly between sleeping and waking, in which ability to function voluntarily may be suspended." Let's condense this: in a trance, you may not be able to function freely.

Here is the second Secret:

Darkest Secret #2:

Manipulators Put You into a Trance.

To protect yourself, you must learn to use Countermeasures to Break the Trance.

All the Countermeasures (actions you can take to break the trance) in this book will make you stronger and more capable of protecting yourself.

Now, we'll view the third Secret:

Darkest Secret #3:

Manipulators Care Nothing for You and Human Decency: They'll lie, cheat, and do whatever they need to do so they win—but their charm masks all this.

Let's return to the example of a Manipulator selling you a house. A Manipulator does not pause for an instant to see if you can truly afford the new house. The Manipulator would neglect to mention that you will not only have your mortgage payment of $900. There will be additional costs: home repairs, property tax, water, electricity, homeowner's insurance, and more. The Manipulator only emphasizes what he or she knows you want to hear: "Look! $900 is better than the $1500 you're paying for rent, which is just going down the toilet. And the $900 is an investment."

Let's go back to **Darkest Secret #1:**

Manipulators make you hurt and then offer the salve.

The Manipulator has you feeling good about the solution (salve) and feeling bad about your current life situation.

How? A Manipulator will make you hurt through questions such as:

- What bothers you about paying $1500 a month for rent? (The Manipulator will use a derisive tone when he says the word *rent*.)
- What is *not* smart about paying rent on someone

else's house instead of investing in your own house?

- How do you feel about your children walking in the neighborhood where you live now?

Do you see how these questions are designed to make you hurt enough so that you'll buy?

An interviewer asked me, "Tom, aren't these good arguments for purchasing a house?"

"What we're looking at is the *intention* of the influencer," I replied. "Let's look at our definition of a manipulator as one who deviously influences someone with no concern about that person's well-being, and who causes harm to that person. If the person truly cannot afford the house, he or she will be harmed by buying it. If the manipulator conceals the truth, the manipulator is doing harm. That's the important difference."

Some friends of mine are ethical and helpful real estate agents who truthfully reveal the whole situation and help the purchaser achieve her own goals.

In this book, we are talking about another type of person; that is, unethical Manipulators.

* * *

In any given moment, we need to remember the tactics Manipulators use. We will focus on the word D.A.R.K. so you can remember details easily and protect yourself from Manipulators.

D — Dangle something for nothing

A — Alert to scarcity

R — Reveal the Desperate Hot Button

K — Keep on pushing buttons

1. Dangle Something for Nothing
What do conmen and conwomen do to seize your

attention? They make you think you're getting a "steal."

I recently saw a documentary in which a conman on a street in England showed a toy that looked like it was dancing. This fake product was actually dancing because of a hidden, invisible thread. The conman was dangling something for nothing. The Entranced Buyer thought he was getting something worth $20 for only $5. That was the trick. The Entranced Buyer felt that he was getting $15 extra of value for his $5. What the Buyer really got was something worth nothing. Similarly, I know someone who purchased a copy of a Disney movie from a street vendor in San Francisco. She brought the copy home and it was unwatchable—and the street vendor was never seen again.

An old phrase goes, "A conman cannot con someone who is not looking for something for nothing."

How to Protect Yourself from
"Dangle Something for Nothing"

Stop! Get on your cell phone and talk through the "deal" with someone you know who thinks clearly. Go home. Think about it. Do some research on the Internet. Listen to your gut feelings. If the salesman or conman is too insistent, get away from that Manipulator. Get quiet. Have a cup of water. Cool down. Break the Trance!

Break the Trance and Identify the Crucial Detail

Earlier, I mentioned that a Manipulator puts you into a trance. An added problem is that we put ourselves into a trance. For example, as you read this, are you thinking about your right toe? Most likely not (unless you stubbed your toe recently). The point is that we only focus on a tiny percentage of what is going on in our life.

Around fifteen years ago, I caused myself trouble because

I put myself into a trance. I discovered that under certain conditions, friendship can make you nearly deaf. Here's how: I was producing a song for a motion picture. A good friend was singing backup in the chorus. Because of our friendship, I wanted him to sound great. I completely missed the Crucial Detail. In this kind of situation, the Crucial Detail is that what truly counts is how the lead singer sounds! I made a song that I could not release. What a waste of time and money! I had put myself into a trance.

In any situation in which the Manipulator is "dangling something for nothing," we often fall into a trance and miss the Crucial Detail. The most important detail is not that we're saving money if we order before midnight tonight. What counts is whether the product creates a lasting, crucial benefit in our lives. And is the benefit of the product worth the cost? Some people even program themselves to make mistakes by saying, "I can't pass up a bargain." The bargain is not the Crucial Detail.

Secrets to Break the Trance

This is the process of B.R.E.A.K.S. It will help you remember the proven methods to break a trance.

B — Breathe

R — Relax

E — Envision

A — Act on aromas

K — Keep moving

S — Smile

Secret #1: Breathe

Remember *Secret #1: Manipulators make you hurt and then offer the salve.* The Manipulator wants to put you into a state of being that fills you with a sense of urgency and anxiety.

Oh, no! I'm going to miss the sale! Stop this highly vulnerable state. Take a deep breath.

End of Excerpt from *Darkest Secrets of Persuasion and Seduction Masters: How to Protect Yourself and Turn the Power to Good*
Purchase your copy of this book (paperback or eBook) at online retailers
See Free Chapters of Tom Marcoux's 47 books
at http://amzn.to/ZiCTRj

ABOUT THE AUTHOR

You want more and better, right? Imagine fulfilling your Big Dream.

Tom Marcoux can help you—in that he's coached thousands of people: CEOs, small business leaders, graduate students (at Stanford University) speakers, and authors.

Tom is known as an effective **Executive Coach** and **Spoken Word Strategist.**

(and Thought Leader—okay, writing 47 books helped with that!)

** *CEOs, Vice-Presidents, Other Executives, Small Business Leaders:*

You know that leading people and speaking at your best can be tough.

Tom solves problems while helping you amplify *your own Charisma, Confidence, and Control of Time.*

"Tom Marcoux coached me to get more done in 10 days than other coaches in 2 years."
– Brad Carlson, CEO of MindStrong LLC

Interested? Email Tom at tomsupercoach@gmail.com Ask for Access to the *Special VIDEO:* "3 Deadly Mistakes to Avoid for Your Next Speech—and 3 Surefire Methods."

You've heard that you need to tell YOUR STORY well, right? (We're talking about brand, product, or profile for a job.)

The San Francisco Examiner designated Tom Marcoux as "The Personal Branding Instructor." Why? Tom has helped thousands of clients, audiences, MBA students express their own **powerful Personal Brand**. Tom helps **you communicate powerfully so people trust you** and gain what you're offering (product, service, an idea!).

"Tom Marcoux coached me so well that when I faced a high-level prospective client, it was amazing. It was unbelievable how easy it felt to me. I wasn't nervous because Tom guided me through all the rehearsing. Tom emphasizes *'Words – Strategy – Rehearsal.'* I was more-than-ready because we had worked through all the possible scenarios. Tom also empowers me with his expertise with *building a unique and compelling brand:* logos, language, media releases, speech-writing, videos and more."

– Tim Cox, the Business Systems Strategist

As a **Pitch Coach**, Marcoux is an expert on STORY. He won a Special Award at the EMMY AWARDS, and he directed a feature film that went to the CANNES FILM MARKET and earned international distribution. Tom founded PitchPowerFest.com (Also see GetTheBigYES.com)

You need to give a great Speech. How about a TED Talk?

"Tom Marcoux has coached me to make my speeches compelling and powerful. He's helping me prepare my TED Talk. Do your career a big favor and engage Tom Marcoux the Spoken Word Strategist." – Dr. JoAnn Dahlkoetter, author of *Your Performing Edge* and Coach to CEOs and Olympic Gold Medalists

This is YOUR OPPORTUNITY. Apply for a FREE Breakthrough Strategy Session with Tom Marcoux at tomsupercoach.com/breakthrough. See the VIDEO.

Tom Marcoux says, "Because of my unique coaching methods, I emphasize with my clients: *You will achieve more than you believe.*"

"Tom helped me unearth deeply emotional and humorous moments in my speech to move the hearts of the audience. He was there for me unconditionally. He went above and beyond anything that I expected. During every interaction that I had with Tom, I felt that I learnt something profound.

I highly recommend for anyone who wants to give a great speech that you work with Tom Marcoux as your Speech Coach and Spoken Word Strategist." – Krishna Noru

As a CEO, Tom leads teams in the United Kingdom, India and the USA. Tom guides clients and audiences (LinkedIn, IBM, Sun Microsystems, etc.) in Extreme Confidence, leadership, team-building, power time management and branding.

> "Tom Marcoux has been an NAB Conference favorite [speaker] for six years. And he is very energetic." – John Marino, Vice President, National Association of Broadcasters, Washington, D.C.

One of Tom's books rose to **#1 on Amazon.com Hot New Releases in Business Life** (and in Business Communication). A member of the National Speakers Association for over 19 years, Tom is a professional coach and guest expert on TV, radio, and print.

Tom addressed National Association of Broadcasters' Conference six years in a row. With a degree in psychology, he has presented as a guest lecturer at **Stanford University**, DeAnza College, and California State University. Tom teaches Authentic Leadership Communication & Authentic Marketing at Sofia University, Palo Alto, California. Over the years, Tom has taught business communication, designing careers, public speaking, science fiction/fantasy cinema & literature and comparative religion at Academy of Art University. He is engaged in book/film projects *Crystal Pegasus* (children's graphic novel) & *Jack AngelSword— Jenalee Storm* (urban fantasy).

Tom provides *A.C.T. Coaching* (Assess, Create, Trim) and *T.O.P. Coaching* (Transform, Optimize, Power-communicate).

With his unique background as a trained feature film director, actor and screenwriter, Tom will role-play with you so you're ready for the tough meeting and even tougher speech or sales presentation.

> "Using just one of Tom Marcoux's methods, I got more done in 2 weeks than in 6 months." – Jaclyn Freitas, M.A.

"There aren't enough adjectives to describe how powerful a coach Tom is. He's not only wise and insightful. He has a heart of gold, and he helped me in ways no other coaches could. When working with Tom, I grew in many ways and continue to have his coaching words in my head as I make daily business choices. I'm so grateful for my time with Tom. Anyone who has the opportunity to work with Tom is blessed for sure." – Junie Moon Schreiber

Consider Tom Marcoux's Online Course **The Introvert's Formula to Get Clients**. Send an email to TomSuperCoach@gmail.com

Become a fan of Tom's graphic novels/feature films:
- Urban Fantasy: Jenalee Storm / Jack AngelSword
  At Facebook.com type: "JenaleeStorm"
- Science fiction: TimePulse
  www.facebook.com/timepulsegraphicnovel
- Children's Fantasy: Crystal Pegasus
  www.facebook.com/crystalpegasusandrose

See **Free Chapters** of Tom Marcoux's 47 books—visible at online retailers.

www.ingramcontent.com/pod-product-compliance
Lightning Source LLC
Chambersburg PA
CBHW030842210326
41521CB00025B/672